JOSEF HANZLÍK
SELECTED POEMS

Josef Hanzlík
SELECTED POEMS

Translated by
EWALD OSERS
&
JARMILA & IAN MILNER

BLOODAXE BOOKS

Copyright © Josef Hanzlík
1962, 1963, 1964, 1966, 1967, 1972, 1981, 1986, 1990, 1993.
Translations © Jarmila Milner & Ewald Osers 1971, 1993.
Foreword © Graham Martin 1971, 1993.

ISBN: 1 85224 124 1

First published 1993 by
Bloodaxe Books Ltd,
P.O. Box 1SN,
Newcastle upon Tyne NE99 1SN.

Bloodaxe Books Ltd acknowledges
the financial assistance of Northern Arts.

Cover reproduction by V & H Reprographics, Newcastle upon Tyne.

Cover printing by J. Thomson Colour Printers Ltd, Glasgow.

Printed in Great Britain by
the Alden Press, Osney Mead, Oxford.

Contents

POEMS 1981-1990

Acknowledgements

Acknowledgements are due to the Arts Council for providing a translation grant for this book.

Some of the translations by Ewald Osers were first published in *Three Czech Poets* (Penguin Books, 1971).

Acknowledgements are due to the editors of the following publications in which some of these translations first appeared. For translations by Jarmila and Ian Milner: *Landfall* (New Zealand), *Modern Poetry in Translation, New Writing in Czechoslovakia*, edited by George Theiner (Penguin Books, 1969), *The Oxford Book of Christmas Poems*, edited by Michael Harrison and Christopher Stuart-Clark (Oxford University Press, 1983), *PN Review, The Poet's Lamp*, edited by A. French (Canberra: Leros Press, 1986), and *Stand*. For translations by Ewald Osers: *Contemporary East European Poetry* (Ann Arbor, USA: Ardis, 1983), *Contemporary Literature in Translation* (Canada), *Daedalus Poem Cards, London Magazine, Modern Poetry in Translation, The Observer, Outposts, Panorama* (Prague), *Partisan Review* (USA), *Slavonica, Sport* (New Zealand), and *Stand*.

The translations are selected from the following collections by Josef Hanzlík:

Foreword

The poems of Josef Hanzlík bring the reader directly into the contemporary world. He first published in 1961. Since then, seven volumes have appeared and he is now considered one of the most gifted poets of his generation.

Until its suspension in 1969, Hanzlík was the poetry editor of *Plamen*, the literary monthly of the Czech Writers' Union. The poems selected here represent his work of the last four years, and the earliest seem particularly youthful, inclined to wordiness and to broad ironies which Hanzlík manages rather as if they represented his passport to cultural manhood. But the fluency and energy are unmistakable, and at the centre of many poems there is a real and difficult subject: political violence. Killings, mutilations, stiflings, beheadings occur in poem after poem, and are connected in some way with people in authority. Hanzlík uses dramatic monologues by invented or legendary or historical *personae*. A man appointed by Robespierre to glue guillotined heads back to the bodies vindicates himself with the crazy reasonableness of a concentration camp subordinate on trial for atrocities. An Armenian tyrant explains that after a vision of God ('his lips compressed in wrath') he stopped persecuting the Christians, and started persecuting the heathens. The Innocents put to the sword by Herod intone his argument that by killing them he saved them from the 'boundless sufferings' of life. Perhaps the most interesting is 'Judas (To Christ's disciples)', which makes a slightly ambiguous use of the Marxist attitude to Christ's pacific strategy. In a post-Crucifixion attack on the disciples, Judas presents himself as the genuine revolutionary, the only man brave enough to commit and provoke violent deeds. Thinking Christ knew what he was about, he relied on the eleven to whip up the people in His support. Having tipped off Caiaphas, he also arranged the crown of thorns and 'the heavier beams for the cross', only to see everything backfire because the disciples didn't come up to scratch.

> For I
> relied on you you gentle vipers
> to use the power of the Word to unleash in the crowd
> a protest a longing for revenge a longing for murder

Graham Martin's article first appeared in 1971 as part of his introduction to *Three Czech Poets* (Penguin). Ewald Osers' postscript (see page 12) brings it up to date.

> I hoped that apathetic mob would sharpen their knives
> pick up the stones that there'd be slaughter
> which would burn Jerusalem to the ground and like a blind dog
> race across the frontiers

At first, it's an effective speech. Then one remembers that a real Judas would have *made sure* that the eleven knew what he was about, a piece of forgetfulness which makes nonsense of his claim to revolutionary competence: who more ridiculous than a machiavellian who fools his own side? The fable, in sum, doesn't altogether express the intended theme: how to act morally in an immoral world.

But Christianity seems to matter to Hanzlík. Both the Judas and Herod poems are not unsympathetic towards Christian pacifism, while in 'The Postilion', he attacks Christian supernaturalism with the energy of a Protestant moralist denouncing Rome. A folk-tale in form, the poem relates how the postilion arrives in the village 'where live the Anxious and the Fearful and those Waiting for Grace'. When they stretch out their arms in supplication, the postilion chops them off at the shoulder. Then, leaving a line of mutilated believers, he drives off with a sleigh full of bloody arms. But again, the metaphor doesn't quite carry the meaning. The poem ends with its eye on the amputated limbs, not the deluded villagers, and the satirical blow at the public target seems also to release, or perhaps to cover, an inward preoccupation with the imagined violence.

This applies, to some extent, to all these satires: the public theme is partly a rationalisation for a more complex impulse which Hanzlík doesn't explore. But in this respect, the later poems are much more satisfactory. Though not gloomy, they reflect the disappointment of many hopes, and the broad, confident ironies have disappeared. But the feeling is more open. In 'Prickly rain...', there is an openly admitted degree of panic at the loss of future directions:

> Feverish beginnings
> ending with a bang
>
> Small roots of grass striking out wildly
> Somewhere up Somewhere down Somewhere else...
>
> Endlessly long ago
> rust first got up early
>
> Endlessly far away
> from anywhere to anywhere

Allusive imagery replaces dramatic rhetoric, and the tone is personal, direct. Similarly, in 'Christmas Time', the Christian symbolism is more subtly used, providing both the bland public rhetoric of the official festival and the core of values which calls it into question.

Hanzlík's energy, inventiveness and capacity for growth are all signs that he is a poet of whom more will be heard. What is admirable about his work is his determination to write about his own world in terms of his own response to it, and to create a language accordingly. So far, both have their evident simplicities, but history seems already to be taking care of that, 'working' as Hardy says of his ironic God, 'evermore In its unweeting way'.

GRAHAM MARTIN
1970

Postscript

Since Graham Martin wrote his introduction in 1970, Hanzlík has had four major collections of poetry published. There was a break in the aftermath of the Soviet-led invasion of 1968: not only was *Plamen*, whose poetry editor Hanzlík had been, suspended in 1969, but Hanzlík himself had no immediate hope of being published in the new conditions. Not only were the anti-totalitarian allegories of *Clap Your Hands for Herod* too obvious to be missed, but a few days before the actual invasion Hanzlík had published a fiercely patriotic (and grimly prophetic) poem, 'Behind the Anthem', in *Literární Noviny*.

Not until 1972 did his next collection, *Euphoria Land*, appear. It is tempting, but probably too facile, to seek a connection between the political events of, and after, 1968 and Hanzlík's development as a poet. But I think that his post-1968 poetry differs from his earlier work. The savagery of language and imagery has now been internalised – not lessened but stripped of its former aggressiveness. There is much greater philosophical depth in his work now. And there is, more often and sometimes surprisingly, a lyrical note in his poetry.

Josef Hanzlík is not an entertainer. He is a serious poet and deserves to be taken seriously.

EWALD OSERS
1993

POEMS 1962-1966

The Lamp

Before my father went to sleep
he always put on the lamp.
Quietly he would lie
in the shy and steady presence of the light.
My father was blind,
he did not see the light,
knew only that it was near,
the switch told him light existed,
he sensed its dry electronic taste
and the feel of light was for him the feel of the living world.

My father had no eyes
he could switch on and off,
but what people think they see behind closed lids
he also saw.
Grave and motionless he lay
and beneath the skin
his body pulsed to the tides of blood and flicker of nerves.
The lamp was shining.
The light touched my father
and he breathed the light,
drew it in by mouth and through his pores
and the light ran through the tangled arteries and veins
flowed into the heart,
flooded the hot darkness of the brain.
And then he saw things as the eye sees them
in their raw tormenting shapes and animal reek.

He saw his own days and the days of those he did not know,
saw burials and the angry rain,
saw the reflexes of a boy's first fears
and again the months without work and my hungry words,
he saw the wormy bellies of dead fish and of legless children –
and you cry O the filth of war –
and he saw my mother,
complete, nothing missed, with red-chapped hands,
desperately erect. The lamp was shining.
And my father looked into the face of those
who against the wall still stood erect,

saw wailing dogs and wild burning horses,
saw smoke climbing heavily to the sky and it was the smoke of
       human flesh,
and he saw those who with eager songs of homecoming
returned to die on the paving-stones of Prague.

The lamp was shining.
And father stepped into his workshop,
again lived through the scurry of changing shift, the whirl of spindles,
the cog-wheels' gentle rhythm,
saw the tensed jaws, taut sinews, unyielding movement,
glimpsed again the chalk-scrawled manikins,
emblem of the child's world of play,
the secret of a girl's blush and the long-cast coupled shadows,
he saw the world in its raw tormenting shapes,
saw the passionate meaning of the human act,
the shame, the hate, the crazed hunger for life,
the lamp was shining,
my father breathed the light,
his body lay all open to the light
and the light passed through him utterly,
he sensed its dry electronic taste
and the feel of light for him was the feel of the living world.

I sit on the bed where my father slept,
I look at the things imprinted with his image,
and at night when the dark is deepest
I put on the lamp.

[JM/IM]

The Fiddler in the Old People's Home

The lining hangs from his jacket
his shoes are thirty years old
And Orpheus plays
Behind his back a radiant shrub
with the dark name rhododendron
There stands Orpheus legs planted apart
intently listening
what birds are these that sing in his hands
On the seat someone holds his white stick
for Orpheus is blind
and only a few children standing near
behind the old women and the old men
know that Orpheus is not of this world
that he belongs to their hiding places
to their dreams and visions

Orpheus plays
his fingers turn stiff and yellow
but Orpheus does not see the age of his hands
behind his lids tall slender Orpheuses play
they play solos at flower festivals
and on the promenades of watering places
where Beethoven and Mozart used to stay
and Orpheus is intently listening
what birds are these that sing in his hands
a ceaseless coming and going
Orpheus does not see the age of his fingers
he plays
and only the silent children know
that he belongs to their most secret hiding places
to their visions and dreams

[EO]

To the Builder of a Baroque Church Well

It happened when the polished ribs of your skeleton
were flaunting their silence. After the air-raid
the church peeled on the instant in syncopic typhus
and everyone heard the dog's whine of the dying organ.

Then the bent-grass grew through the frame of your well.
Nowadays at noon a vagrant child sits there with a spider.
At the bottom potsherd and earth stifle the water – and you sleep,
sleep in a rotten wig under the leaves of a dream-book and fractured
        linden trees

But during the green nights when the algae shine,
your limping feet overtake your Rimbaud drunken boat,
and chase after it in the well's spring.

You scoop up the pale water in your winged palms.
And the moon leads you with arms outstretched as if to the day
when people will again go off their heads for a gulp of spring water.

[JM/IM]

Poem for the Journey

It's night, an incredibly ordinary night.
Like little Ovid the soft rain persistently
writes its hexameters on the window-pane
while on the road below the women loved by long-dead philosophers
idly stroll,
circling the taunting traces of the puddles
and it's all incredibly ordinary,

it's night, an incredibly ordinary night,

suddenly a window opens,
someone shouts exultantly:
Friends, a child's been born
and in a moment we're there and take it in our arms
to assure ourselves the child's alive breathing,
we take it in our arms, pass it round to one another,
lift it high above the planet,
the child sees much further than us, a galaxy or two doesn't matter,
it takes everything for granted, cries out,
scans its fingers, brushes aside the distances,
what's Aristotle's logic to it,
or making war,
with our weeping walls.

The child was born far beyond our understanding,
born with Einstein in its little finger,
has Goethe and Stravinsky at its finger-tips,
has a brain we've never dreamt of,
laughs away our fear of strontium.

It's night, an incredibly ordinary night,
and something special has happened,
a million children were born who like fire-bearers
pass kindling wood from planet to planet,
we cry out with them,
envy them
and say quietly to ourselves –
Let us come to you, little ones,
our palms shall be worthy of your foot-soles,
our mouths worthy of your names.

[JM/IM]

18

The Rubbish Dump

At the rubbish dump on the town's edge
      love my love
I breathed a soul into all things
rusty and twisted
things dead and abandoned
      my girl

At the rubbish dump on the town's edge
      love my love
I gave coal scuttles back to kitchen ranges
and the ranges to the kitchens
I gave things back their former life
      my girl

Blindly the trumpets blared
      love my love
strainers strained fearless tears
horses ran out of ancient lexicons
Who chopped their heads off one by one
      my girl

At all the rubbish dumps on the town's edge
      love my love
I gather the milk-teeth of young horses
I gather the imprints of their hooves
fistfuls of hair from their manes
      my girl

My fingers are bleeding
      love my love
how can I dig down
to what remains in us
to what we have not thrice denied
      my girl

At all the rubbish dumps on the town's edge
          love my love
the child's pure heart soared highest
bit through the wire-fences of this world
and understood...
                    only to forget?
          girl
          my girl

[EO]

Things

In the drawer of my desk
I have my birth certificate
some silver coins and a collection of postcards
a general's six-edged dagger
and a velvet rose
ugly now though once it smelt sweet

I was reading Andersen
and it struck me: tonight
the things will come to life the coins will ring
postcards catch fire and the dagger
stab the miserable rose

Nothing like that happened of course
dead things don't suddenly come alive

Myself I had to
take the dagger in my soft white hand
and stab

[JM/IM]

The Voice

Above the city the rain still hovers
heavy as the tread of dray horses

In both of us the whip cracks
more blindly
down to the depths of hate
which in the sultry air
under the horses' bellies
we pretend in place of our long-rooted love

I promised you
a winsome colt
and at night I'll bring it from the mountains
but you'll be asleep
that furrow of anger on your brow
now buffeting mine

But you'll be asleep
and like a wandering lutanist
I'll play before the gates of your dreams
until long-dead children
wake up in tears
and the palms of stones grip each other in fear

But you'll be asleep
more unhappy than a procession of Ophelias
breakfasting on the underwater sedge

You won't hear me
sighing like a tendril
you won't hear my voice
released from a butcher's hook
O vox amoris flatibus
O burning voice

But you'll be asleep
and the words
that should summon the whole of you
now

in the sultry air and the swelling rain
are not on my lips
angrily I try
to strike harder
rip and choke
my old inhuman love
usurped by our pretence of human hate

Above the city the rain
tosses from side to side
blind
like us

[JM/IM]

Love

The cog-wheel turns and turns
    tooth for tooth
    tooth for tooth
yes: tooth for tooth

But we two
thank God not precise
thank God not metallic
thank God timid so timid

again and again will say to each other
Today I still
forgive you

[JM/IM]

Variation VI
(Question)

Where are you going? Where aren't you going?
And will you get back dead and well?

Are you as white as the milk of God?
Does Aunt Katherine drink beetle wine?
Did we have one foot in paradise?

Signor d'Amici
what was that story about the Lombard sentry?
Shall I too be shot through the heart?
In what flag will you wrap me?

Did you lock up when you left the house?
Did you switch off the light?
So no one else should come
and make himself at home?

Did I ever see anything
in any country anywhere?
Will a dream like that bring luck?

Shall we change water into poisoned wine?
Will the air kill us as it strikes us?
Shall we fall under the wheels of a car tonight?
Can death do its job even without glasses? Can it do it by heart?

Can you hide in yourself
so that you can teach him to sing
even before birth?

Can I hang every other child by the dangling rope?

Is truth in lying stockings
a true lie?

Can one overtake the past
and return to the future?

Will I die?

[EO]

Variation VIII

Understand that you cannot escape
all your solitudes
are only temporary refuges

At the age of five I had a lover
At the age of five I had a mistress
But a real one!
He (she) loved me with milk-teeth dug in my shoulder

I can repay you
only with mouse-like tears
break some bread into my milk and go

I saw you naked at the bottom of a river
in a picture-book country
If only a dream like that brought luck

Do not wake the sleep-walking children
their candles will set light to the roofs
so we should have one worry the less

You can beat her as much as you like
you can kiss her with hatred
you can drown her you can tear her hair

you can use her

My dreams are too loud
something shrieks at me with large letters
straight into my ear
I can't make out a word

Don't forgive me
go to bed with a book
in which I deceived you

I shall return to you like the winter
but make no mistake
all I bring is sad rain

[EO]

26

Variation IX

I walk in the fog
afraid of my hands
they point steel at living men

Wedge driving in wedge
On the bottom barely audible a miraculous
Head and a stone
which in her sleep presses into her sleep

Squirrels and elms are drying up
around the barbed wire
horror gravely limping makes its round
more transparent than glasses on a dead man

Only don't smile so enviously
your bad luck still clogs my fingernails
my nails in the empty sockets of your eyes

[EO]

Variation X

Go to sleep
compose yourself for yourself
finish my wine finish biting your nails
finish your loving in your dream

Her favourite toys
were the fat keys of lean houses

Our sleep goes off to sleep
Our falling asleep
is falling asleep beyond the mountains
Our dreams are dreaming outside us

Don't throw the clay over her
open the lid
she'll say listen
to my heart not beating

The words which came to me with you
are irretrievably lost
Whatever words came to me
are irretrievably lost

If only you swallowed
how you lie in my stomach
If you swallowed her
how she hates us

Don't put nonsense in your letters
love surely goes through the clay
I'm killing in me all your flesh
I'm yellow I'm dying to spite myself

Be quiet
I forgive you everything
in non-love of ourselves
I know no brother

[EO]

Variation XIII

The silence of one who speaks
The speech of one who does not answer

Any metaphor
The dog of silence
the cow of silence
the bark of dog silence
the severed eyes of the cow of silence

From childhood I have been tortured by the thought
that a dog will attack me in a shirt as hairy as a dream
and that I will be helpless

There under the blossoming tree
where I used to lie with you my love
where we cut the hanged men's fingers off for luck
where I buried my eyes for seeing
and my ears for hearing
there under the blossoming axe my love

Spit it out
spit me out
do you hear
never take me in your mouth again

God whom you are forever seeking
won't even come to your funeral
the god whom you have driven away
sups with you every day behind your door
waiting for you to let him in

I had a sister she was thick in the knee
she had to die so I should not stammer

Go heat your soup
no soup is eaten as cold
as it is served

Rave on
don't come round
we are digging your grave
like a bed of roses

And finally: kill the stone with your head
throw it out scrape off the scales
the pigeon heart you'll cook from it
will like myself have eyes on top of the head
and teeth behind the tongue

[EO]

Variation XVI

Ugliness that stands in my eyes
like chewed straw from boots

Ugliness that is beautiful
like the Titian-red of any aesthetic knacker's yard

Ugliness that is real
like the sheep rotting in the rotting belly of the sheep

Ugliness that is neither anguish nor joy
that flows from anguish into joy

Ugliness that is in me
as I am in myself and none other

[EO]

Variation XVII
(Abductions)

Wolves carry off affectionate children
the river the clay of the dead
fire a letter with a lock of hair

The stone runs with a broken bone
Teeth carry off deceived intestines
The dog hides out with a severed glass eye

The belly carries off the gums and a foot
glass grips grazed skin
raw liver makes off with mildew

The whitewash hides a purloined sleep
The brine has trapped two spiders and some plumage
grass conceals tetanus

Puss mixes with Cinnamon
oil reaches out for oats
the whip carries the window-frames away

Concrete swallows urine
the handkerchief bites the lung
typhoid carries off armpit hair

The bed denies the nail-marks on the neck
crying carries off nocturnal gloves and sorrow
the wardrobe has slammed shut on sister's shirt

The morning rips the tongues out of love's shoes
The wind from the slaughter-house snaps the umbrella's ribs
The violin carries the rope away and with it everything else

[EO]

Variation XVIII
(Menaces)

The rust-brown colour menaces the black
The brain menaces the bony skull
The sawdust menaces the oatmeal bread

Winter is ravenous for a raw heart
Insects menace the bridal bed
The mirror shows its fist to the writing desk

The fire mocks the young oak shoots
cats' heads mock Icarus
the lavatory bowl the funeral wine

The drum menaces Balaam's she-ass
the lame old woman her two-legged grandchild
The wild dog laughs at the feathers in the featherbed

Felt humbles the hare
Lime boasts to King David
Glass hair warns the toymaker

Loam menaces the straw beneath the foals
and children's tears the forms of autumn crocuses
everything threatens everything else

No one is threatening someone
Mud keeps a stranglehold on all feet
Dreams keep the hopes of our old age in check

[EO]

Variation XIX
(Graves)

The coachman digs a grave for the horse
the coach for the traveller
the hen buries a pea

A new grave digs a grave for the old grave
the purple shoots for the yellow potatoes
stifling sobs burying longing

The flame tolls for the candle
the candle for cellar blackness
cellar blackness for childhood

Sun buries fish with the pond
the morning cry flings earth on night's anguish
the knife sings a requiem for the brown bread

Someone is parting from something
Someone has broken a cross over something

The dead have buried their dead
the living are burying the living

[EO]

Variation XX
(Escapes)

Ants flee from fire and hunger
Teeth chatter down to the knees
Rats gnaw their way through the deck

Pots are afraid of red-hot tin
the lame wolf of a hungry niece
Poppy flees from the sickle

Vengeance fears twofold love
love fears nettles between the sheets
the sheets fear fever and death

Anything seeks safety from anything else
The razor blade from rust
rust from honing

The dead move away from a bed of beet
Forgotten cheese shakes at the thought of mildew
Oats avoid the windmill

Man avoids his God
God his Man

[EO]

Variation XXI
(Sometime nowhere)

Start somewhere
Continue nowhere

Somewhere I was small as a doll
like a pretzel like a pencil-sharpener
I'll never go back not even as a little dog
not for a kiss nor for a penny

Borrow my glasses sometime
you won't see anything any more

Somewhere fog blossoms like a white poppy
Somewhere I saw your portrait in white flesh
Don't ever try to get out of reach of my ears
Don't ever cry your heart out

Sometimes they bind the hands as if they were floating
sometimes the necks like dead chickens

I feel as if it were sometime long ago
I feel as if I had no hair
I never asked you for anything – even spittle
I'm here yet somewhere else
Ask for me somewhere in a dream
sometime I'll buy you white poppies for your cheeks

Sometime   somewhere
sometime   never   nowhere

[JM/IM]

Variation XXIII
(Tasks)

What God will frost can kill
wind drowns leaves
arm breaks a leg

Salt sits ready
Starch takes hold
Oil grasps   chokes

Feathers don't deny the fur
The roof won't pardon the dry-rot
Time doesn't wait for fire

Autumn puts up the waitress
winter the innkeeper
Mould puts it over you then and there

Wood entreats clay
The arsonist's children run the wall against their heads
cast swine before pearls

Indifference still rises with the morning dew

[JM/IM]

Variation XXIV
(Psalm for the Dead)

The sun sleeps in the poppy fields
In the winter stoves spiders flourish
The twilight ghost sneezes in children's mouths

You shall have a good sleep

May you sleep long like against the stream
Do not try to cheat the others who are dead
do not spare the children of the living

Do not come back even in darkness
nobody here is going to give you a light
in the stable there is an axe and a rope

nails in the ashes have their countless cares
the soaped-off grime has grudges enough
the raw fish is full of indifference

Cocks are hanging on the village green
from the belfry hangs an Anabaptist
And the privy goes on foot to the emperor

You shall have a good sleep

Nothing happens here
no matter what you dream
Horror pecks horror's eyes out

Do not try anything
everyone is a little better off
without you

[JM/IM]

Variation XXVII

Next time
no memories
of anything

No dreams of happiness toothy smiles
no mutes tongued with unhappiness
no rust   no messages

Now only prosaic misery
only prosaic fear
that tosses your verses underfoot
like peas   like potatoes
like sticks

I really was waking up in time she said
but the bad winter surprised me
I really was dying in time
but the bad summer surprised me

Sighs
Well-spring   parting   growing old
Punctual   arrow-swift
Headlong
Anxiety
Hobnail booted foot-slogging taken for a ride
Making it new   hatred   Well-spring   growing old
Sighs   nothing new
Anxiety
Roof under one's head

Stone that burns wonder-struck
I burnt she said from childhood to childhood
Ashes burnt to the bone
Burn with love for me
My head's burning
Burning bush

Leavetaking that ties knots in your hair
Weariness that nips your toe-nails

Eat quickly   don't fuss
the horses are raw
tears are there by the window
smiles from the coal   love's   behind the ears
perk up   freeze   sing   sleep
grow rounded   stow away for a rainy day wonder
accept nothing   don't choke just strangle cut and slice

hate   bend the knee
poison yourself   bathe in dew
die
lie

[JM/IM]

POEMS 1967-1972

Vengeance

The night bird beats against the bolted door
Unless you've smeared the handle with the blood
of a sacrificed lamb
he will smash the first-born's head against the door-post

But woe unto you if you are marked with blood
having sacrificed your neighbour
in the insolent error
that he is less than you

for then the night bird
will reward your house
with the mark of his friendship

and there will be no grief but you will taste it
there'll be no death
but you will die it

[EO]

The Wound-healer

Wound-healing is my trade Healing of wounds
Robespierre himself that chopper-off of heads
one far-off night entrusted to me
that fruitless task of glueing the heads back on
It's thundery I'm getting sick and troubled
It is an effort now to lift those severed heads
A hand perhaps the wrist-joint of a child
or a fistful of hair
I can still manage to pick-up and glue back to the dead body
The mud's a nuisance How many pairs of boots
have I worn out – and how many ribbons
accepted gratefully as a reward for my service
And rightly so For surely it is not a matter of indifference
if some dead person who adorns our history
is without a head or without nails or whether
his ribs are stove in for world without end
I'd say it matters And looking after the dead
is a more serious task than looking after the living
But as I've said before – I'm getting weak
and dazed so that in the mornings I scarcely lift
my own head from the gutter
where it falls There are dreams and non-dreams for a dream
is what I long for whether sleeping or waking
and what does not come true And in my non-dreams I see all
            the things
which terrify me which depress me
waist-deep in clay All these are lifelike
only more real Thus I see myself
in fields thick with carnivorous grasses
and enormous cabbage-heads which groan
and howl with pain for they are half rotten
And phosphorescent fungi which at midday
raise heads of greying death
and rocking menacingly long in the rhythm
of some strange song that has dissolved like plasma
I'm below ground And sad damp clay
seems to be seething stratified and heaving
until it bubbles and chokes my breath
there's not a blade oh god a single blade which...I'm in heaven

and the rickety trees
which from here grow with their foliage downwards
caress me with their roots with such smooth snakelike gentleness
that I moan insanely I never killed
I only lifted
the bodies from the traps and disengaged them from the wheel
from the trough of the guillotine I would always
lift the heads gently by the hair
and with a rag admittedly not always laundered
I'd dab the neck and on one occasion even
used a chamois leather to polish the glasses
of a certain scientist and only then
stitched the bespectacled head back on
Did I not personally
water that bed of white roses
by the gallows daily
did I not graft and weed to make the place a scene of beauty
where people said their last farewells
I never killed Only very occasionally
would I complete the strangling of the all-but-strangled
complete the breaking of a neck complete the axe-blow
but always only in the line of duty
in order the sooner to mend and to heal
the wound of the dead Why then and by what right
do they invade my dreams – the white
the airless the croaking dry ones
the drug addicts exhaled from the organ pipes
full of self-hate sitting at the keyboard
Why then and by what right do all those heads
winged heads like birds come sweeping down on me
from the phantom realm of tumours and worms
why do they sweep across the low horizon
filling the sky from one end to the other
gyrating now in black concentric circles
around *my* head *I* did not cut them off
I only glued them back...

[F.O]

Tartat III

At the age of fifteen
I first sacrificed to the gods
a slaughtered lamb and a chicken Alas I did not suspect
that even among the gods some are stronger some weaker
some simple some cunning
some forgiving some vindictive – and what is worse
that you not only earn no thanks from mortals
but none from the gods Not only no thanks from the gods
but none from mortals
                    During the first year of my reign
news reached me of rebels in the mountains
who spread faith in a single god Even earlier
my father had some such preachers jailed and with them
a handful of shepherds But now the messengers
were bringing more alarming news every day
of secret nocturnal masses and fires among the rocks
of miracles and many deluded people
who let their children be baptised and refused
to sacrifice to the gods And in the dungeons
with candles and red-hot wires we have meanwhile
persuaded the old men to show their wisdom
and publicly reverence the gods Not one of them
however was sensible and they all died Soon
the people proclaimed them saints
and the stormclouds thickened At that time also
some forty maidens crossed the kingdom's frontier
pledged to the Christian god Along their route
my followers got fewer I sent out my soldiers
and one by one they put the girls to death The wailing
and heart-rending sobs they had to listen to
So not a day passed
without a few heads being cut off as a warning
and the odd house set on fire...
                    One fine morning
happy and weary from a mass of work
I left for Lake Sevan We refreshed ourselves
in heavenly blue and amber-limpid waters
we killed beasts and made our sacrifice
When after prayers I glanced up at the sky

it was suddenly rent by lightning red as rubies
and through the rift appeared the head of the Christian god
his lips compressed in wrath I fainted
and when I recovered to my horror and that of my companions
                    I found myself
turned into a boar I understood instantly
what god demanded On my return
I summoned the prophet Gregory
who had spent thirteen years in an underground prison
and was the only old man of the Christian faith
still left alive His holiness was immense:
He turned his eyes to the heavens and god
gave me back my human form Only my left ear
remained protruding and bristly
a permanent reminder of divine power...
                    All night
I spent in prayer The following day
I summoned my army and allotted the regions At once
the first flames leapt up
in heathen temples and the first executions
took place of those who refused to acknowledge
the one god It took some weeks yet
to convert the country to Christianity because many
wished to remain in darkness But soon there arose
gleaming and mighty Christian cathedrals
many of them dedicated to the old men
whom I had tortured to death and many to the maidens
whom I had killed I myself kissed
the finely wrought casket with the remains of the charming Ripsime
at whose violent end near the palace
I had myself been present...
                    During all the masses
which I forthwith conscientiously attended
and during private prayer in my gilded chapel
I would cast surreptitious glances at the altars
and through the window at the sky
expecting praise or some token because in my country
I was not loved But I lived soberly
made sure the saints were honoured and mercilessly
crushed every heathen manifestation
And after thirteen years
I even released from his underground cell

the blind and crazed heathen priest
who alone had survived his fellows and moreover
had ceased to sacrifice to his gods – we had long
cut off his hands...

                                  But alas to the end of my days
I had to hide that bristly ear
God
never appeared again

[EO]

Judas

(To Christ's disciples)

It's over then You cowardly dogs
you proud, cultured, exalted men with your gentle eyes
and measured gestures and fulsome sentiment
now you spit at me and as from a pulpit
shout Traitor Dirty filthy traitor
For thirty pieces of silver for one night with a whore
he robbed the world of its Light robbed us of the Teacher
You rats Where did you scuttle
as they led Him to Golgotha Where did you shake
with liquid-bellied fear Where in your confusion did you
throw your badges and how many of you like Peter
denied Him thrice You sanctimonious weaklings
did I not offer you
a sword Did you not flee from a mere dozen men
Did even one of you His darlings and His brothers
attempt to shield Him with your own body
Or afterwards when He was tortured in his cell
did you go out among the people calling for help
Were not the people able to decide Surely the people
could have said No to Pilate Let Him be our king
You pharisees You wanted Him
killed For on the corpse the still warm corpse
you built a temple where you would be kings...
                              I'm off
to find a stout branch
and one that's seen so that Jerusalem
shall have its three-day giggle I who alone
was worthy of a place beside Him or after Him
I who had a sense
of tactics and strategy I who did not shrink from
stealing lying even garrotting
for a Sacred Cause I who understood
that I was to use the funds
even for tricks and corruption I who longed
to multiply our property and secretly buy weapons I
who realised that the Master's whole repertoire
of childish miracles and deeds of human kindness
was useless stuff today That today the Teaching

must be propagated by the swifter language of arrow and battle-axe...
                                            And I
had a plan I wanted
the Master to be taken and held in the worst of
the dungeons That's why I thought up
that crown of thorns so that the mob should see
the red drops That's why I advocated
heavier beams for the cross That's why I egged on
that crowd of layabouts to line
the road to Calvary And lastly that's why
I got on to the high priest...
                                How cruelly
he was to have been outwitted For I
relied on you you gentle vipers
to use the power of the Word to unleash in the crowd
a protest a longing for revenge a longing for murder
I hoped that apathetic mob would sharpen their knives
pick up the stones that there'd be slaughter
which would burn Jerusalem to the ground and like a blind dog
race across the frontiers
the enemy would be routed and – why not admit it – a good few
of our friends would inevitably die
But what of it I would unite the survivors
in a great everlasting happy realm of the Faith
O the Master knew well the strength inside me And he realised
that I am more consistent that I am more apt
to propagate the Light For He
had but a name Otherwise a simpleton
and also alas a coward That's why He feared me
and would rather go
meekly like a lamb to the slaughter
Not only you but He too
lost me my fight and betrayed...
                                But the traitor for eternity
for the record of history which as always
has the last laugh that's to be my role
I blood-brother to Cain who was wiser
and braver than the rest for he was not afraid of murder
who was by your forefathers as I am today by you
branded with the mark I'm off now
I don't want to live like an outcast
despised I'm off

That hill up there
looks suitable
All I need is a branch
I have a rope

[EO]

Who's that driving a black cart...

Who's that driving a black cart
through the disconsolate rain
who's that not sparing the exhausted horses
wheels drowning in the mud

Who's that driving a cart
through this landscape with no roadside inns
and no burning pinewood
disregarding the dawnless night

Who's that driving
along this futile road through a drowned world
emaciated to the bone

Who's that driving an empty cart
who but the gravedigger who like the captain
dies last

[EO]

Noah

The last days before the rains
were murderous People were killing
themselves and others The dead were mouldering
and the handful of living were drinking with the publican who alone
still plied his trade His wife
let rooms
haunts of adults and alas
also of children The ark
had long been prepared
I suspected a good deal but certainly not
the worst: while the animals
were kept ready in their pens
while baskets urns and bags
were full of food and while below deck
two sets of sails and everything to preserve life were stowed
everyone thought me crazy and nobody
except some waifs and strays and a lame fortune-teller
who died soon after we sailed
wished to accompany me...
                         Then came the rains
My own sons and daughters
and all relations cut their throats
the rest the old the sick the children
were quickly drowned The waters closed
over the valleys and soon
the hilltops disappeared The ark drifted
this way and that unendingly over a perished world
I was saddened The children suspected nothing
and below decks played happily
with the young of the animals When after many days
the water began to recede the ark
got stuck near the summit of a mountain
which subsequently was named Ararat The earth
dried quickly for the sun returned
within the reach of childish arms We looked out
to see a multitude of dead fish
but also revived flowers and grasses
I collected a few things and with a pack of children
went down the valley The horror of that silence

defies description As soon as I had knocked a house together
I set out with the older boys
for a tour of the neighbourhood Weeping
we climbed over human bones
and the remains of dwellings The children asked
How is it no one knew
How to strengthen the dykes did no one apart from you
know how to build ships did no one
want to live did they really all
want to die or were they afraid
to resist death and finally
did no one apart from you
remember the weakest those
who have to be looked after
like flowers...
                    And I bit
my fingers till they bled from impotence and grief
and after my return for days on end
for sleepless nights on end I dug the soil
and planted seeds and watched over
the children and the sleep of the livestock
in desperate self-punishment for the thousands of dead
the only survivor and hence
the only one apprehended
the only one apprehended and hence
the only one guilty
here
before the children
who being without merit
are also without guilt

[EO]

The Postilion

In a ringing frosty night the postilion arrives in a blue and white piped coat and a tricorn hat rich with tassels

And the postilion blows his horn and the eight pairs of horses which draw his fabulous sleigh ring with silver

And the postilion comes to the villages where live the Anxious and the Fearful and those Waiting for Grace and at each sound of his horn and each note of his silver bell the Anxious and the Fearful and those Waiting for Grace run out into the street for the postilion is bringing them Grace

And the postilion places Grace into their outstretched hands and as soon as an outstretched hand catches hold of Grace the postilion cuts it off with an axe right up to the shoulder and flings it into his sleigh

And thus he distributes Grace and thereafter cuts off the hands clutching Grace – the hands of the Anxious and the Fearful and those Waiting for Grace down to the last man in the village for he too believes that for him an exception will be made

And only in the forest behind the village does the postilion sling out all those severed arms from his sleigh removing from them those decorative wrappers with the unmarked paper so that provided they are not too badly blood-stained he can use them for others

[EO]

Elegy

To be able to unlock your inner locks so that you cry out
but with joy To be able to unlock you so that you sing
but not from grief So that you recognise in me a fellow prisoner
but in love... To be able to unlock your breast

But so far I only ceaselessly wrench the seven locks
and the chains which guard you close to my heart though alas silent
and fleeing from me deeper and deeper – like a fledgling swallow
fleeing from the rain which loves it too much not to kill it

To be able to unlock you And then the iron cracks in the joints
and in bleeding fingers I suddenly grasp you
by your mouth and hair like a person drowning

And you free yourself without a word and like a sleepwalker go
                softly
as if bearing a cross... And behind you runs your blood-red trail
those leaves gone mad with longing

[EO]

First Fiesta

Everyone who promises to take part
in today's fiesta
will receive a bouquet

The others will get only words

Here she comes like a flower like the white poppy in her hair
white
with a bevy of girls

You're not mistaken it's she
Hortensia who alone may pass by without spot of the blood
trickling for her from our mouths and eyes
opened
by a hair pilfered from a child's curls

and it's she
Hortensia whom I'll never see in the past
and have never seen in the future

And I sit down under the threshold of the summer-house
where she's writing me a letter
sealed with tears
for it's me she loves
and it's her I love

once again it's the humid soil that puts me to sleep
a little known winter animal
that wakes during winter
and there's a rhododendron bush
cheeping dismally under its load of snow

I dial a number and the receiver says
don't come to us God it's cold here
like in a morgue
I'll return your books by post

finally I enter the summer-house
Hortensia is asleep in an armchair
fully dressed
lifelike

I go back to my burrow
the summer-house roof over my head

under the snow
benches and tables lie overturned
on the fences Chinese lanterns dumbly grieve
like heads stuck on stakes

Then I get drunk
and sing a brief song of spring
full of gay madcap flowers

[JM/IM]

Second Fiesta

Four black horses
searching the ground
for our lost horseshoes

They were silver
and so small
we remember sadly

Where shall we go

The black horses churn up the ground

Where is that tiny lake
from which we drank
when shoots of rye barley and wheat
sprang from your delicate fingers
and irises from your eyes

The lake does not sing
it's choked to the bottom
with dead swans

Where is the rosebush
which bloomed even in winter
blazing through the garden

Where is the garden sun with its red hair
entangled with the hair of wise children
and where is the garden moon
fleeing
from the dove-like moans of lovers' grass

Let us saddle the four black horses
let's not forget the bread
the water in the hollowed gourd
we have a long night's journey back

Only let's hold out
let's hold out as the black horses hold out
quite soon
we'll be living only on strawberries
and on wine
only on kisses
and on milk and honey

only on faith
only on lies

[EO]

Clap Your Hands for Herod

We
little children in our shirts
long ago washed clean
of bloodstains
have gathered together
as we were instructed
and are making ready to greet King Herod

For us the massacred innocents
a special place was kept in heaven
Here there are woods
plentiful with undergrowth and game
and grey caves we may creep into

We the smallest of the dead
once believed in our ignorance
that King Herod
was a wicked man
who had us killed
from mere brutality and lack of heart

But we were told:
Look at the woods where you live
even the smallest song-birds
snap up insects coloured like the rainbow
to be fattened
for a wild cat's jaws
the little snakes swallow mice
big ones rabbits and hares
and when the wolf that devours sheep
falls sick he is torn to pieces by his brothers
And so it is with the plants and flowers
one strangles another's growth
grabs its piece of earth
and place in the sun
Worse by far
is it among human beings
who besides animal malice
have hatred one for another

and the cunning
to perfect their power to kill

These things they said to us
and we pale-faced little angels
gasping in terror
cowered closer to the tree-roots
and gave thanks
that here in these woods thirsting for blood
we were not really alive

and they spoke further:
There is no love among men
anywhere in the world of the living
But King Herod
loved above all else
you little mortals white as the lamb
and therefore freed you from life
that you might be spared
its limitless horrors
Be grateful to your deliverer
and should he come among you
greet him with clapping and song

And there were some among us
who cried out
that in life there *is* love
their palms kept the memory of it
and that King Herod
was a foul murderer
who ought to be quartered
with a butcher's axe
and his parts
thrown to the wild beasts
but others of us
stopped their mouths
for we were full of joy
and gratefulness towards the king

and eagerly we listened further:
Give thanks that you were delivered from the world
that valley of tears

where what they call justice
is a blind whore holding scales
who has turned all the openings of her body
into wells of the plague
give thanks to King Herod
who has saved you in the fullness of his love

and we wept
tears of remorse for the lies and slander
we had come to believe
and lifted up translucent hands
in thanksgiving for the truth shown to us

and we are gathered here for the last time
around the sacrificial shrine
preparing to sing praise
and waiting to clap hands
for Herod

who is coming to kill us all over again

[JM/IM]

Festive Times

All night long the rain failed to dowse
the cemetery lights   For the dead
have matches soaked in animal fat
Festive times   All Souls time   And in front of a wall

love trips up love   Festive times
All Souls time   And she says: I've got the creeps
Sing... And he answers: I saw grass
stifled by gas... it was blue   Faint-heartedly
she kisses him   while the statues
wag their fingers: Yes kiss on the heart but for God's sake
not with the teeth... And the dead

make the most of permissive night and sing for the living
as in the Old Testament – arms outstretched
heads up

[JM/IM]

Geometric Discoveries

Never-ending geometric discoveries
Triangles are outdated   Fashion
brings graceful squares
and trapezia   Above us in heaven
Archimedes doesn't abandon his compasses   Da Vinci
builds his siege machine   We laugh
from the cold   But a mouse
runs through a maze more quickly than a man
Things for disbelief and belief in non-things   Then
we'll melt down our swords or at least
dig over the graves   Somewhere in the fields
we will conceive new children We shall inherit medals
and great expectations   Sad birds
will sing for the light-hearted   High up in the gardens
we'll discover the first infirm point   A dot
that after a long look changes
into seven suns   The seven suns' dot
and more of love's word play   The miraculous
breathing of the body into a boy's soul
Red rain   White blood   You name it
Even a woman can be created   But never
from a gouged out rib

[JM/IM]

65

The hard winter...

The hard winter is killing off the rabbits in the tree-roots
Below the crowns
a cloud of icy sparks wheezes and lower down
the snapped branches sway
like the hanged

Warm my hands since I too
lie on the ground by your roots
and am lightly clad

Hungry uneasy the rabbits and hares
gnaw the tree that protects them
and the trunk dies
And again the frost's glass splinters
encircle everything as in a dream
and you can't find the tracks
along which the dead animals' spirits depart

Where then to run
except to your home under the rock
unshaken by storms
and the air meant for breathing
turned to glass

And hearing you call I run off
leaving footprint after footprint marked by my blood
footprint after footprint
raw freshly killed snow

[JM/IM]

First in her sleep...

First in her sleep stab her
in the throat with the twin-bladed knife
Then when she screams
muffle her mouth and her nose
to choke her
Then with swift strokes
flay her alive
tear out bleeding fistfuls of flesh
lay bare the bones
When she dies
cut out her tongue
The last word on it will be
your hatred
Don't lose it
plant it in spring
it will sprout
with a rust-red spongy flower
swollen with nectar

[EO]

Autumn Crocuses

I wish you a dab of white and green
a dab of healthily poisonous perfume
a dab of sadly joyful shade in the forest
this I wish you
for your birthday

a dab of poison that would be beautiful
and always at hand

so you should be mortally afraid of everything

so you can try to survive it

[EO]

Rain

It rained as though I dreamed a double dream
I was afraid
for all that firewood
so pointlessly
carried into the forest
that it might rot and moulder

and it

really rotted
really mouldered

it's really glowing
with nocturnal phosphorescence
with poetic paralysis

it really leads the children
deeper into the forest
so deep
that they can never
return unmarked

[EO]

Silence

Silence like a blow
with axe or word

Silence like a knife
at the throat

Silence like a scream
from rock to bottom

Silence as from a gun
as though into a drum

Silence like the first syllable
uttered after death

Silence already
and silence until

[EO]

Flower-bed

Plant here ferns and grass
strawberries nails tears and tamarisks
posts in the fence hard bread
the uttermost part of the world and myrtle with water
plant lilies here
and soft shade
and mainly your fallen-out
pulled-out knocked-out
teeth
so there may grow
many sweet lips
many lips laughing and singing
so there may grow many sharp teeth
to bite on a sentence
to crack a nut to suck a wound
to sink them
at last
into a throat

[EO]

Above the earth...

Above the earth blue sky
And here
choking fumes stifling
As if I did not exist
as if I merely appeared in a dream
which comes to me full of stark terror
almost daily And if there's reason to fear
one's own lips
and also one's heart yes mainly the heart
then I'm afraid Autumn is here
kicks and leaves are flying about
as in a forlorn game You give me your hand
which is blue and cold
and which uneasily and almost thoughtfully
now grips my throat Yes that day long ago
there was dew in my eyes –
now only evil senseless salt
the salt of hurtfulness which stings
Now dawns a blinding darkness
in that dream
Above the earth blue sky
And here?

[EO]

Prickly rain...

Prickly rain like midsummer roses
striped tiger's rain

In sobs and tears
stone stifles stone

Sharpness nailed to pricking eyes
A thousand things like a desert

Feverish beginnings
ending with a bang

Small roots of grass striking out wildly
Somewhere up Somewhere down Somewhere else

A rainy scarf on a riddled throat
Mutual anxiety

Take a knife to the pain
take a knife for carving and boning the pain

to make sure it is digestible
to make sure it does not stick in tongueless mouths

Rain like crusty bread
like laughing lead

Cinnamon axes of a resin-perfumed net
of ferns over silvery moss

the happy terror of childhood
like the play of dragonflies with a drowned man's ear

Endlessly long ago
rust first got up early

Endlessly far away
from anywhere to anywhere

[EO]

Christmas Time

Sweet Christmas time is coming
in gentle Euphoria Land
and a very merry new year is approaching

Here they are not preparing limbs for breaking
or breasts delightful as oranges –
only to stub out matches on them or cigars

Here all will be merry
and the children in silent fear in silent terror
are awaiting even their unpromised presents

Here brittle frost will crunch happily at night
and from on high soft snow will settle
obliterating all traces without trace

Here everything will happen charmingly
as in an operetta: after a glass of wine Orpheus will sing
and Eurydice will dance for the gentlemen

Here in their midnight nostalgia they'll remember
even those whom fate has mercilessly snatched away
and officers will dry their tears with their sword pummels

Here all will be merry – and lines from the Bible
will be quoted with relish And here in front of the camera
they'll plant their cross and once more save the world

Here the echoing voice of the bells rises over the landscape
so solemnly so much in divine exaltation
that I shall not forget it while I live

Here all will be solemn all will tremble
as if laid between the leaves of flowers
under candles shedding burning drops of peace

Here will be such mirth as befits
a country without a god a country without people
here everything will be eternally delightful

in Euphoria land

[EO]

74

Tall Houses

Even in this sulphurous land
outside the gates of an unwanted paradise   In the land of insults
and dust   In the land of lament   In the land of despair
Even in this unending land where the end is approaching
In this promised land which I never promised you
and where we are nevertheless walking alive and naked
because we belong to the betrayed
Even in this devastated land which devastates us too
let me remind you of the dream of tall houses

There used to be an orchard here
and in the orchard a wealth
of winesap apples
There used to be the scent of orange-blossom
I would lie down in it
on the grass which gently hid
your laughter and your loosened hair
as if for next time   There too was your dream
of tall houses slender as flowers

It is raw and the words are departing
from our unlaid tables
And all alone and all uncertain
I flounder in your breath as in a sudden
and deliciously painful shower
I stretch my hands to your petal-ringed eyes
as if sinking to the bottom of a glittering forest
with urgent mouth I move
from the soles of your feet to your lips
and from your lips to the soles of your feet
as if I were trying to suck
your anguish and mine from your burning depths
I search for all of you in all of you
so as to return you to the dream of the tall houses

For we are wandering through a sulphurous land
locked within the gates of an unwanted paradise
For we are wandering through an endless land
where the beginning and the end of the wall have been joined

and the broken glass on top does more than wound
For we are wandering alive and naked
and only in our dreams does the pavement open before us
full of insults and bitterness and ambushed blood
to let us pass on sympathetic clay
and the loving grass of our children's childhood

For there used to be an orchard here
and in the orchard a wealth
of winesap apples   For here too was your dream
of tall houses slender as flowers
in a land
in a land whose name I forget
in a land
whose name might be Love

[EO]

Fairy-tale Christmas

The door open to the courtyard
inside the table set
outside the last cries of game
inside the bed made
outside the final secrecy of fish
on the table the two of us
naked
olive sprays behind our ears
knives and forks at hand
beaks hungry for a taste
claws clenched

The door open to the courtyard
like on the stage:
Polonius fumbling with his sword in the curtains
rather Hamlet fumbles with his sword
in the curtains and pierces
the soured rancid belly
and now jingle bells and a snow boat
in the shape of a swan
and now anything can happen a miserable death
humbling hate and prettified love
out of a fairy-tale
unreal

The door open to the courtyard
the ceiling's caving in
the lining pokes out the ribs are bare
of the fairyland house
is the play going to start?
yes   only more green and sepia moss is needed
so that both of you can step quietly
from backstage with the wedding knife
amber noose and of course
the poisonous apple

The door open to the courtyard
in a cradle
a fairy child   sweet little sailor

wind in the window and a pheasant head downwards
in front of the window lonely and maudlin
we understand each other with teeth and fingernails
buzzing in the eyes   glare in the ears
to whom do I give myself   to whom do you
in this unreal house full of trap-doors

The door open to the courtyard
deep in dream like the dead
we embrace the fairy-tale tree
burning from the crown
and somewhere a still drying drop of blood
somewhere a coral bead   somewhere a shirt and potsherd
lick up and grab what you like   tear it to bits
in this fairyland house
batter the joints stick the feather-bed together
before we take off for the mountains

[JM/IM]

Lullaby

You fall asleep, my love, like the trees' greenness
and in the dark the mountains float
up towards the mountain peaks on the high sky

You fall asleep, my love, like the trees' greenness
and within me the softest sounds are hushed
so as not to wake you   Now only childhood
may soundlessly sing
into the golden shell from which years later
we hear the ocean's ring

You fall asleep, my love, like the trees' greenness
and silently
desperately
into your dreams there falls a star
of wishes I did not fulfil for you

You fall asleep, my love, like the trees' greenness
and on the traces of your touches
I now gaze on my hands
which long for you   From them tomorrow
some mute white grass will spring

You fall asleep, my love, like the trees' greenness
and somewhere in the moss and in the waves
sleep will be rocking you and distant from us all
you now flash only like a knife
that's shot up over the abyss   And thus alone

from us and from yourself thus without help
a step away from death and within touch of life
thus you, my love, like the trees' greenness
on the night's threshold when I cannot sleep
because I love you
and love the anguish born of our love

you fall asleep, my love, like the trees' greenness
you slip away from me in slender music
and it would only take a word

from me to call you and to bring you back
a single word, my only love
a single word
which I won't utter

[EO]

POEMS 1981-1990

The Fire of the Tower of Babel

I. *The Report*

This strange and incoherent report
appeared to come to us with autumn
in the wordless language of nostalgia
this report
appeared to come to us in the howling
of blizzards
or in the confusing strings of the melting ice
in vertigo
and in moments before death
this report appeared to come to us
with the blinding thirst of an August sky

This report   this account

This report fused into the stone
together with the hand that wrote it there
This report vainly swirling up
the glassy surface of the sand in the Gobi
This report creeping up stairs
towering empty from nowhere to nowhere
under miles of water
on the dead seabed

This report   this warning

This report in a language that does not resemble
any of the languages we speak
This report whose fragments were known perhaps
to the builders of the pyramids and ziggurats
this frightening and accusing report
these torturing and destroying tears
over the devastation in the gardens

This report   this account
of a human hand which started the fire

II. *Babel*

The heat was unbearable
We retreated step by step
our eyes dead from horror
whipped by the flames
which waved like the scarlet banners
of a victorious war

To the creaking of hurtling beams
and the roar of cascading stones and bricks
to the helpless cries
which blended into an anguished chorus
of crazed singers
we watched how our brothers
painfully flew out from walkways and windows
like birds on fire
how they vainly spread their burning wings
how they dropped to the ground
into the rubble
fragments of stained glass
and darkening blood

We retreated
swallowing tears of shame
tears of guilt
and on our hands with which we wiped our foreheads
remained the dust of scorched eyelashes   eyebrows   hair
as future dust of our brethren
as future dust of their children
conceived but not yet born
as our own future dust

We retreated like blind men
step by step but tenaciously
leaving before us
the trampled
struck dumb and spasm-racked
but not for a moment losing sight of
that collapsing
and yet still firework-like
spurting   upwelling   cloud-reaching

burning
flower of a tower

for we were the ones
who caused this ruin

III. *Babel*

And this we had wished:

to build a temple in the shape of a tower
by which we'd join our open hands with heaven
That malicious idea
of peering into the gods' beds and guts
was not attributed to us till later
We were building our edifice for man
Each one of us saw his son or grandson
gazing down with pride from the tower's walkways
on a desert made fertile   on dew-moist grapes
on orange groves
on lakes with waterfowl
on girls scarcely able to carry their armfuls
of olives and dates and pomegranates
Each one of us saw his own eyes
in the eyes of those children
his own love
so generously and gently spread around
for their loving

IV. *Dr Michihiko Hachiya, Hiroshima*

It was a calm and balmy morning
and from a cloudless sky a leaf was slowly falling

In my own garden shadow yielded to shadow
with great and delicate ceremony
as in an ancient drama

And suddenly I saw two flashes of light
The garden lamp jerked up

and its stone shone blindingly
In the raised dust as in some monstrous dream
slowly and gently
the house sank down

As an involved spectator of the event
I did not notice the pain of the blood
that was leaving me
I did not hear the words
with which I called my wife

Then we fled
and I nonsensically apologised
to the dead head over which I tripped:
I'm sorry
I'm so sorry!

We were accompanied by flames and silence

V. *The Report*

Perhaps only a shadow's imprint on the stone
some dried-up river-beds
incomprehensible drawings on cave walls
symbols and signs
to which we find no key

For history
is too inexact
too lacking in non-loves and loves
as we ourselves

Perhaps only those words gone with the wind
syllables no longer uttered by anyone
the vanished names of children   names of things
the vanished sweet cries of gentleness and anguish

vanished verses
which maybe will ambush us one day
brutally   unexpectedly
like that rusty nail
in the burst lump of coal

like a death-cry
like a warning
like a sharp rending exclamation mark

Perhaps we'll read those words one day
words whispered by the desert wind
words held behind the teeth of ocean depths
perhaps we'll read them
words of human happiness   of a human miracle
that has slipped out of human hands

Perhaps those names
of children
songs
love
and reason

and the names of horror
the names of hate
and the names of reason that have escaped reason

Perhaps we'll read them
in that wordless report
of the nostalgic autumn wind
in the cracking of the ice-floes
in the vertigo of dying

Perhaps we'll read them

in time

so that our own words are not
one day discovered
for future poets
as something unexpected and incomprehensible

on the sea-bed
or under sand dunes

[EO]

Winter: Snow Queen

In some frosted swansdown
in some Brussels lace
it's her delicate feet
slim as a flute
fair enough to kiss like fallen snow
from shadow to shadow
from wrinkle to little wrinkle
softly probes my skin
with trained physician's fingers
while snow settles
on Prague's ancient pantiles

more sensitive than instruments
with a smile of bitter triumph
oh yes and knowing
she tests and slowly confirms
like the brittle and miraculous
melting splinters of snow
those fruitlessly evanescent cells
and the more wearily beating heart
that fruitless (like steam over Christmas yearnings)
flight of my years
and decades

[EO]

Blue Landscape with Hamlet

Yes there is somewhere an azure coast
yes there is somewhere an ultramarine distance
yes there is somewhere
a grey and white and silver blueness
of pigeons' wings
and cornflower longing

yes there is somewhere a colourless shadow
of my screaming fingers
extended
searching groping
surrendered
to life or death

[EO]

Here in this fairy-tale...

Here in this fairy-tale
I'm now the last of your princes
And suddenly everything's here
this slowly extinguished sun
like strange copper above the peach tree's branches
your cruel shadow
limping like this comparison
amber fear in your eyes
and the chill of your frosted laughter

and suddenly I am here
naked and ludicrous
under the leaves of the mulberry tree
from which my friends now
sadly distil their mulberry spirit

[EO]

Album

What remembrance
what stone stuck in our eye
what sweet death will we two take with us?

Will it be touching
like children's talk to children?
Will it be armfuls of leaves
and cheerful clothes and shoes?
Will it be lost letters
or pure bleeding pain?

Yes perhaps they'll throw us as crumbs
to the swans on the lake   Perhaps they'll only throw us
to the stray dogs   Perhaps they'll just wall us
into the piers of the bridge
which will arch over the dungheap
Yes
perhaps we'll get away yet with honour
and save our skin

[EO]

Traffic Light

Slender
in the gold-flecked spring or autumn wind
a blade between her teeth
and countless smells of blades in her hair
wind-blown and full of sparks
like a halo

Slender as a blade
with grazed knees
and wild joy in her eyes

Slender
herself still a blade among rustling blades
on a boy's bicycle
in a spring or autumn sweater
the handlebar in impatient hands
she invites us

anywhere into the distance and of course
into childhood

along the road on which she knows
she alone
is allowed

[EO]

This is the dream...

This is the dream in which the frail sepia
and dark red leaves of the trees
fall to the ground
while the mad wind weaves you
like a spider's web

But my hands
can't grasp and strip the words alive
and my feet no longer hear
even the small roots of the grass

[JM/IM]

Episode

As there is earth wind or bell
and that old sad smile on your lips
as there is a rock a tarn and then a dream
from which I return to you lame and walking backwards
as this is all: pewter and hate
algae plague and tenderness
and a broken-winded horse
that carries the story round and nowhere

so I'm here
with the timeless silver in my eyes
longing in my palms
and crystals in the liver

so I'm here
(like the red fog in your last dream)
stifling your complaints
and cutting short your cries
of self-defence...
                    Here the sand blows
like the grey wings of a fleeing pigeon –
and that depth of blood bones lips
the depth of my fingers clenched in yours...
Day has come
like a flower
blue and white behind our fingernails:
and snakes devour the soil
thorns move close to one another
from the bog sprouts seven-leaved love
the frantic camomile yields to the nettles
lead embraces its sulphur

and the one who suddenly drowns irrecoverably
in the pavement's crevices
among the flowers
and the footprints of children dogs and fog

is me
here as if for the last time

or the first
and yet too late

like your death
from which I wake in the morning
like my birth
from which I shall not wake

[JM/IM]

Epilogue to a Novel

You're getting up to go
still don't understand
still warding off the thought of it
you want to explain
shrug it all off
with a wave of the hand

but the lid's already on

now you can only curl up into yourself
only patch it over

you hold on to the lungs
and the heart runs away
you put the stomach right
and the teeth fall out

All that's left is adding it up
money days and acquaintances
to come down a peg
find a roof over your head

sit down
wait

[JM/IM]

Stamp Collection

Across the stamp collection
(not graced by the legendary blue Mauritius)
childish eyes sailed off to silver islands
in overseas possessions of the British or the Portuguese crown
and of dreams
they sailed off with Columbus on the Santa Maria
they sailed off with Magellan and Vasco da Gama
as though Captain Cook were waiting for them far away

Across the stamp collection
childish eyes gazed into the vacant eyes of the Egyptian Sphinx
they blinked in the glare of the Sudanese desert
and the smoking San Miguel volcano in El Salvador
across the stamp collection
childish lips first tasted
the magic intoxication of tom-tom words:
Guinea Borneo Fiji Madagascar
Cameroon Congo Transvaal Philippines
Pahang and Labuan Hong Kong Hyderabad
Lourenço Marques...
for if there are such places as the Orange Free State
and Prince Edward Island
if there are such places as Victoria Land and the Ivory Coast
then surely there is also the Land
of the enchanting Queen Mab
and a country of elves and sprites and trolls
where William Tell's young son
with a smile
demonstrates a dangerous big weapon
and an apple safely pierced by an arrow

Alas the time comes all too soon
when the collection must be viewed with adult eyes

First we behold the emperor
in the majesty of his side-whiskers
and the glory of sixty years of peaceful reign –
followed at once as on a stage
after their death

by the Heir Apparent Ferdinand with his wife Sophie
then artillery cavalry biplane
and the warship *Viribus Unitis*

Then come the surcharge stamps
in favour of war-disabled and war-blinded

And on the next page nothing but inflation
in Germany the postage runs to milliards
you go out shopping with a rucksackful of notes gone crazy
and the hungry bread fits into your pocket
In the bars
jazz now holds sway
and in the fashion houses the flowing line and flat breasts
and on the cinema screen silent grotesques

George Grosz draws
accurately as for an atlas of anatomical monstrosities
who goes to work at five in the morning
and who sicks up champagne on wine-red
plush

But we have peace
between two wars
and elegant (if vulnerable) Zeppelins
take off to all parts of the world
Josef Ressel re-invents the ship's screw
and Viktor Kaplan his turbine
the Danube Shipping Company offers excursion trips

Hans Christian again laments
the Little Mermaid
Goethe makes friends with Schiller
Beethoven with Bach
and Henri Dunant unendingly
repeats his success with the foundation of the Red Cross...

And if he hadn't already received
the Nobel Prize
As if mankind hadn't had enough of glory
as if those hundreds of cholera hutments and tons
of paper bandages

soaked through with pus and blood
hadn't long been burned

For twenty years will pass
and all will start afresh
and in this no-longer-childish collection
except for the changed names of satraps and of kings
except for the perfection of technology
the technology of killing and the technology
of stamp production:
the casualties on crutches and the war graves
will be printed in more delicate colours
And the inflation that follows will set a new record;
Hungary will print a stamp
in the value of 500,000 billion pengö

Let us not shut our adult eyes
with smug cowardice and neurotic phobia
to those pages in the collection which hurt
to the jolly butchery to the bloody carnival
of Governments-General and Protectorates
to the death-mask
of Reinhard Heydrich

Yes after the war from the collection
a shriek will rise from Lidice Ležáky and Oradour
the acrid smoke from Majdanek
and girls will faint
at the unending horror of names
carved into the walls of the Pinkas Synagogue –
Just as if the fire had never ceased to burn
under the gentle soles
of the Maid of Orleans

But among the stamps of our own day
Blériot again flies over the Channel
Zátopek runs a breath-taking finish
a sleepy Madame Curie discovers radium
and Professor Einstein writes a very simple formula
for an incomprehensible theory of relativity

In the stamp collection
just as in the Anna Seghers story
around a table in an old Prague café
we find the embittered satirist Gogol
the slightly mad E.T.A. Hoffmann
and with a barely perceptible smile
the youthful lawyer Franz Kafka

Altogether
in the collection of peacetime stamps
poets and novelists meet one another
like on some secret thriller journey
by Orient Express:
François Villon and Jean Arthur Rimbaud
Sergey Yesenin and Walt Whitman
Daniel Defoe and Ovid
Mark Twain and François Rabelais
Anton Chekhov knowingly watches
as with a gypsy fire in his eyes
William Shakespeare
personally acts in his comedies
on the world that is a stage

Ah yes on those peacetime stamps
the Ferris wheel in the Vienna Prater
revolves unendingly
under the circus tops the Marinarella thunders
and from the sky comes the wingbeat
of millions of Picasso's doves

On peacetime stamps
championships are held in archery
and in the royal game of chess
the fight goes on against malaria and worldwide hunger
for the transparency of water and the air
for the survival of dolphins and mankind

yes on those peacetime stamps
there are international rose shows
and amusing rallies of veteran motor cars
on peacetime stamps
Dr Albert Schweitzer

again builds his hospital at Lambaréné
the heroes of Jules Verne novels
set out upon their difficult and exciting journeys
in balloons submarines and on camel-back
accompanied by animals and dwarfs from Disney films

on peacetime stamps
Grimm fairy-tales are told
and the sea-bed is explored in bathyscaphes
on peacetime stamps
there is a plethora of humming-birds flowering cactuses
and wondrous rainbow-like aquarium fish
of prehistoric beasts or orchids bivalves
glittering minerals
and children's drawings

on peacetime stamps
Arthur Honegger listens to Bizet's Carmen
and Shostakovich
to Wolfgang Amadeus Mozart's Magic Flute

on peacetime stamps Robert Koch
still struggles with tuberculosis and Alexandre Dumas
laughs with his musketeers at Don Quixote's misadventures
on peacetime stamps
keyed up and tense for victory
like the antique Discus Thrower
Charlie Chaplin enters stage-left
and from the right that darling of the girls Gérard Philipe

On peacetime stamps
shine the bright colours
of Chagall's Lovers from the Eiffel Tower
of Gauguin's South Sea beauties
of Goya's Naked Maya and Dürer's Rosary Feast
the luminous light of Morstadt's Prague

the blinding blackness
of Guernica

on peacetime stamps
people build canals and mountain sanatoriums
open-air museums and polar stations
on peacetime stamps
the age-old message of Altamira comes to life
while giant telescopes
listen to surmised messages from the stars

on peacetime stamps
Vostoks Telstars Lunas and Mariners flash past
moon buggies and lunar jeeps set out
on peacetime stamps the dust is slowly settling

on man's first footprint on the Moon

on peacetime stamps

a peace that can't be peace between wars
peace before the last war of all

mankind's last peace

in this once childish stamp collection

on this our childish planet Earth

[EO]

Moment

It's twelve o'clock Central European Time
and the girl feeding the pigeons
seems to have stepped out from a precious painting
from an ancient dream
for the sun is shining from up high
and the air's vibrating warmly
and the high-rise blocks around the girl and the pigeons
seem brittle and translucent
like special-occasion porcelain cups
and the eleven-year-old girl in a check skirt
with eyes shining from up high and warmly and preciously
is casting crumbs of bread to the pigeons
like the Host

and the beautiful pigeons
with attentive trustful eyes
flutter and strut around the girl
like gentle friends
like flowers and the air
and the sun

and the girl brushes the last crumbs from her palms
smiles into the pigeons' eyes
who wait a moment longer

and then
one by one reluctantly fly off
as though luring the girl
to follow them
into the warmly vibrating air
to the sun shining from up high

and the girl
gently opens her arms
embraces the porcelain buildings with shining eyes
and
flies up

[EO]

Sixteen

And she reads
with earnest diopters on each eye
a cruel sweet fairy-tale lie

In her girlish bed a plush teddy-bear
is bored as if in a club of English lords
he has the eyes of a man-about-town

Yes
as though he'd just chalked his billiard cue
in the Tsarist officers' club

Yes
in the world of the Red Queen
in the world of Alice
in Wonderland

And then
the girl moves
between the bathroom and her little room in a high-rise block
in her nylon pyjamas
as in a transparent sonnet by Pierre de Ronsard

the points of her breasts
like the sharp shivering hunger
of snow-trapped birds
like those last
those unuttered
words on the tongue
like fairy-tale gooseberries
under which lurks a snake

[EO]

Sci-Fi

Ruby lights
atop the high-rise blocks
shining in the night like fiery stones
in the rings of a six-fingered hand raised

towards a Faustian and inky sky
towards a sky of dark steel blue

Come on, fingers start talking
Come on, sky change from violet to lilac
and from steel blue to ultramarine
Come on, electronic eyes of the buildings start talking
not only to us living here on the planet Earth

but also to those on the stars
who unobserved have long been observing us
as a thoughtful surgeon regards a dying man

Come on, cry out in a ruby cry
in an interplanetary or interhuman code:
You're waiting in vain   You won't see it happen
We are not dying
we are alive

For time moves on
and our small sky is suddenly bright
with the cross-fire of nightmare rockets
into a lovely morning

Before my eyes the kindergarten lights up –
the first fluorescent tube and the first
palely glowing windows

And those pale windows
are suddenly lilac-coloured
and that Faust suddenly sings only
of a wild rose

because from the high-rise blocks emerge
our children with glass reflectors on their sleeves:
STOP!

We are alive!
We shall long be alive
We'll even find the ever-living
living water
And finger to finger we'll pass on
touch to touch
the electronic human ruby fire
incomparably more eternal
than the ephemeral eternity of the stars

[EO]

Autumnal Words

October wind like Savonarola
rips up the incunabula in the trees
and sienna and rust
and ochre
        black
           and Bordeaux
flee from the delicate illuminations
into the lap of clay

Some words
which as yet have no name
some words as lithe as lilies
huddle together as if in love
as if in anguish
maybe white words or azure words
maybe words like screaming silver
maybe words like silenced death

Ah what printshop owner and what publisher
ah what Johannes Gensfleisch Gutenberg
ah what printer with a saffron soul
will set these words of autumn
on silken tissue paper
on gossamer-light paper
on hand-made paper
with the watermark
of two mute hearts?

[EO]

106

Picture in a Golden Frame

Suddenly I see you as if in a picture
by a summer and Sunday painter:
slender and brittle amidst crystals of sand
with closed eyes
with a long golden light of ringlet hair
down a defenceless body
along which grains of beach glistening like gold
jealously and enviously moan
as water moans in sweet golden anguish
when it touches
your soft locked places
and as the wind wails in golden torment
as it flows through you
as it flows out of your lips
like a straying gondolier
like a genie flying out of a bottle

Then I begin to be enviously jealous
because I see the self-assured golden
aristocratically slender fingers of the sun
knowing their way about you
better than I
swiftly unlocking you
with just a golden hair or hairpin
and I am jealous
because my lowered tear-filled eyes
have for an instant looked
into the confident golden eyes of the sun
from which you are not even hiding now
from which suddenly you aren't concealing anything
because they goldenly are quite at home
not just below your eyelids firmly closed

but also in the monstrous infinite darkness

beneath your golden rosy oyster-shell-blue
like dragonfly wings evanescent
like golden butterfly dust impermanent
skin

[EO]

Mirror Poem

You have to read the poem together before a mirror
        and watch your eyes
              be sure
      they're still alike
           still flicker
      with the conch tones of tremor and tenderness
          read the word eyes
      and read your eyes above the printed page
          like opening flowers
      like a pool where flowers drown
          search them
      for the last tint of unshielded pigeon-grey
          the last touch of azure
      the last glint of emerald lightning
          read your eyes
      and be happy in your love
      it's not too late
      never too late for those
          who read a poem together

[JM/IM]

Air Show

This year's air show at Letňany airfield
was held in bad weather
A strong wind blowing and many showers
from a grey sky
Among the spectators lovers
hugged happily under umbrellas
designers of light summer dresses
were in despair
But I admired
the incredible aerobatic game
of jet fighters in threes or sixes
soaring and diving
in a bizarre minuet or polonaise.
When
they flew off the television screen
I ran to the balcony
and watched them in the real sky
returning home
Already beyond range of the cameras
but still with the same symmetry
For breaking it
would mean death

When it was over
I turned off the TV
in my flat close to the airport
and glanced
at the postcard
tucked under the glass top of my desk
Pilot Alphonse Pégoud
standing there in a leather jacket and riding boots
in front of his monoplane Blériot

Though French his moustache
strangely reminded you of Kaiser Wilhelm
He looks grave right leg slightly bent
goggles over his peak-cap

The postcard was issued by the Prague Ladies' Section
of the Central School Foundation
and bears the inscription:
Pégoud's take-off in Prague
25 and 26 December 1913

Letňany airfield didn't exist then
and had no air shows
Pégoud hovered over the city's Letná plateau –
to Prague onlookers his stunts were miraculous
He not only dived
and rolled but also
was the first in the world
stunningly to loop the loop

He flew in a famous but long outdated type
or rather
in an outdated but famous one
Because in the same monoplane
already in 1909
Louis Blériot had crossed the Channel

Pégoud stands in front of his machine
which looks as vulnerable
as our children's models of long ago
made of plywood and parchment paper
His plane's front wheels
must have come from a bicycle
The engine is half exposed
the canvas fuselage held together by thin wires

Everything is as light as possible
as if Alphonse Pégoud were to become
airborne on his own

He's not smiling
his lips aren't parted like a film star's
he doesn't smoke a cigar
into the lens of the folding hand camera
he trusts himself
believes he'll put on a good show

Only he has no idea
that in a year there will be war
and he'll be flying over the front lines
without loops without applause

Only he doesn't know
that in two years
he'll be shot down
during a reconnaissance flight

That he is going to die in the debris
of a French air force biplane
bones crushed
and hair aflame

That he is going to die
just like his brilliant admirer
Antoine de Saint-Exupéry
twenty-nine years later

During a combat flight

Yes during a combat flight
The author of looping
and author
of *The Little Prince*

Because war likes to murder
those we loved in childhood

On 12 June 1979
the little known Bryan Allen
twenty-six years old biologist from California
flew across the Channel
in a self-propelled plane
seventy years after Louis Blériot in his engined monoplane

Light as thistledown
his sunlit graceful
long-winged Gossamer Albatross
flew for two hours and forty-nine minutes
over the waves between Folkestone
and Cap Gris Nez

Yes this young doctor in spectacles
(no goggles for him)
proved that Daedalus was right
proved that Icarus did live
that he had a chance
and hope
like any man who wants to be free
and happy

The air show at Letňany
ended hours ago
Now it's night maybe close to dawn
The TV screen
doesn't bring any more live transmissions
by satellite
even to the Antipodes
All is dark in the Czech Lands and over Europe
Yet birds will soon be calling
children waking from their autumn sleep
going off into the fog
to their nurseries and schools

Above fog-bound Prague
nothing flies
The Airport's closed
passengers in the lounges
spend moody hours over drinks at the bar
ringed by smiling hostesses
and the Faustian splendour of tourist posters

But somewhere in childhood memory
somewhere in the memory of coming old age
Louis Blériot starts his flight across the Channel
and in no time Alphonse Pégoud
waves to Prague's amazed spectators on the Letná plateau
pilot Saint-Exupéry writes
his undying lines about tamed love
and the young man from California
tongue scorched by thirst
pedals and pedals to show
that poetry is not just a dream

Maybe this young man should also crash
during a test flight?
But do we have to count up the wars
like the Louis on the French throne?

The Letňany air show
has ended
The aerobatic flights have returned to the hangars

In strict symmetry

Breaking it
would mean death

[JM/IM]

Bed-time

First I wish you a soft fall into sleep
like on moss or some honeyed slope

I wish you shut-eye long enough and sound
that you may float as far as fairyland

I wish the finest fairy-tales in which
dragons lurk and many a wicked witch

as well as princes in their silver armour
of whom dragon and warlock stand in fear

Let Aladdin's lamp never fail to beam
its magic light upon you as you dream

May the golden apple-tree and its fruit thrive
and the third brother find the water of life

and with it also hidden priceless treasure
His petrified brothers may he to life restore

The end must be joyful: a wedding scene
May Goldilocks – that's you in dream –

be happy with her prince so brave...
Yet not forget she has a mother's love

Since in dream-land there are rivers nine
you must be sure to choose the very one

that quietly flows by night to fairyland
and in the morning brings us home again

[JM/IM]

114

Afternoon

Somewhere under a tree in the afternoon
a child lies asleep

The sun is shining
and the television screen explodes
with stored-up blood:
yes
the sky still rains terror

In the branches a bird chirps
and somewhere under the tree in the afternoon
a charming child lies asleep

Here
in your anxiety
the shooting doesn't stop:
Light as jasmine petals
or blown kisses
missiles fly air-to-air
surface-to-surface
or surface-to-air and air-to-surface
and water-to-air
and ground-to-water
or water-to-ground
Missiles quick and sure as love
from eye to eye

The bird flies from the tree's branches
and the child wakes up —

and any anxious words
stop suddenly in the throat or on the tongue

and any paranoid hate
ends in a blind alley of the heart
any missile
is electronically guided back

because a bird chirped and flew away
and a child woke up
somewhere under a tree in the afternoon

and the tree is a blossoming apple tree
and the chirping bird in flight
is still alive
and the beautiful child now fully awake
is your daughter

her eyes happy
and searching

[JM/IM]

Winter Love

This pale blue flower
refracted in a cross
at the rim of Bohemian
crystal
fell from the balcony
in a fog of despair
a telegraphic act

a flower
like my hand
curved
behind your neck

hand that burns to throttle
or embrace you

and will not let go

while on the balcony the winter snow
is falling
silently white
like our blood

[JM/IM]

Nursery

Children don't sleep

only tiptoe away from us
when they hear the azure flutes
they leave to make sure
they still know all about
their fairy paradise
that everything is in its place
and the doors open to them

Children are waking up –
to the wonder of sun-dazzled blinds
in charming closets
and summer-houses in dark corners of the garden
And there secrets pop out:
unfinished words
masked kisses as in an operetta
and dreamed up animals
Children are waking up
as the flowers laugh

And children are laughing
as the flowers wake up
as the sportive rain
thrums clear
and amber-light like peas
on a window-sill
and on the blades blanketing
the grass world's childhood

Children are laughing
as only they can

[JM/IM]

Loneliness

Like people who come to me
with limpid autumnal eyes
collars upturned
in the deceitful afternoon rain
blacking out the day
under the torsos of roadside trees

like people who come to me
on the way from a surburban cemetery
huddled in each other's arms
in a shadow-play of umbrellas
– What's been happening, friend?
– And what's on your mind, child?

Like people who come to me
since in my heart dusk's also falling
they know it they sit down
at the foot of the unrumpled hotel beds
in unknown cities
in forgotten years
amidst fading music
in tear-stained transient pain
they sit with me
in kindly wonder
their limpid autumnal eyes
fixed all night on the door
at which no one is going to knock

[JM/IM]

Nursery at the End of Winter

In the garden of a neoromantic villa
decked with fanciful oriels and turrets
the children dance among silver spruces

They don't know when Baron Ringhoffer lived there
nor Freiherr Ritter von Skoda
they don't understand the emblems in the coat-of-arms

Tipsy from a transistor's music
they shout and dance shawls flying
eyes glowing like supernovas

and on their upturned faces
eyelashes and lips
the late February snow melts

flake by flake
like countless tears of laughter
like casual happy kisses

A sodden flag hangs from the villa balcony
the girl teacher struggles for calm
Don't be so rough you'll hurt each other

but they don't care for wisdom
nor for state holidays with flags
too happy running wild

dance and dance again their dream from Andersen
and voice our own delight
there in the February snow

they don't know that their natural acts
go with the meaning of history
squeezed to them drop by drop

nor do they expect thanks

which lapse
and therefore endure

[JM/IM]

Little Mermaid in Karlovy Vary

Haltingly silently the smiling leaves fall
with a more and more metallic
taste of blood in the mouth
like after a duel

haltingly silently the hair is silvered
unobserved but with a secret sigh
and kindly apology:
excusez-moi –
I wanted to stay a child for you

haltingly silently night surprises me
allows no escape

haltingly silently love leaves me
as if I couldn't survive twice
the same pain
as if more and more misty faces
flowed in the river of love's hurt
as if the river's flow of our love's torment
were constantly slackening lost
in going back to the long ago
back to the underworld –

And suddenly the chimes of Sunday morning
as in the white and green of cruel old Russia
And suddenly in front of the window a forest wall
woven by the October gale lurches
over the roofs up to the clouds
alive like a Provençal gobelin
in bizarre medieval armour
and such seductive flames
burning impatiently to ashes
and in no time
the feathers fall from the knights' helmets
and the gold from the standards

In the languor of night at the girls' villa 'Hetty'
harsh aggressive voices resound
confused singing and cries
the pulsing blood of seventeen-year-olds
and under the balcony the filigree town disappears
in the valley like a sinking Titanic
whose lights must go out for ever

And then a small gentle mermaid
enters my heart
floats into the hardened veins
and retreats to the one brightness
the lightning flash the glitter
of my Ultima Thule eyes

And the band plays for very life
Baby hands up
give me your heart or your life
give me give me your heart

it will soon be morning
in the tower wine-tavern of Charles IV
the headwaiter taps out in Braille
tommorrow's menu
the saffron waitress laughs
her quiet all-knowing laugh
her artificial eyebrows flicker with life
and her empty thighs dance on their own
as though the world was still under the baton
of Johann Strauss

The small sea nymph
leads the sad aching eyes
through the silent café Elephant
where only the hundred-years-old Ulrike von Levetzow
sleeps in despair above a marble table
as if on a poet's grave

because the mermaid knows
that today October 15 in any year
an angel will climb Mt Everest
and perish in the descent

And the little mermaid knows
that every morning at the spa
she floats up in the rising mist
from the cooling springs

like the electronic numbers of cardiographs
like the psychedelic haze of falling asleep
like a pool like a painful futile memory

in the waning tremor of consciousness

before this rainbow transparency
before this fragile shell
this porcelain plaything
is shattered infernally to the mute sky

like fleeting human sadness
like this Werther town
like this infantile planet

...Hans Christian Andersen

[JM/IM]

In the Heavenly Darkness over the Town X

It is 20 hours Central European Time
Above the town an empty leaden sky
in the first third of October
Night is descending on the streets
the night of lovers stray cats and hotel bars
or murderers and police patrols
In the streets of the town
eyes blinded by neon
and the glitter of shop windows
cannot see as far as the starless October sky
they don't perceive the little red coral
winking solitarily like blood
intravenously trickling drop by drop and hastening
to prolong someone's unique event

The little coral is urgently winking
Its flashes tread on the darkness
like children's bare feet tip-toeing
The aircraft is on a scheduled flight
and the air hostess announces in broken English:
'We're overflying the town X'

Ah yes in the town's streets
in corners in the parks in back seats of cars
in borrowed bachelor flats
and under the arches of the bridges
lovers are writing the Stories of Countless Nights
murderers are testing their razors on a hair
and junkies with ampules and powders
crawl out of their holes

Ah yes in the aircraft
which hums softly like a summer meadow
people with a glass of Ballantine coffee and a cigarette
are watching the town below them
those clumps and cascades of light
exploding shining spreading like a bursting supernova
in the Great Magellan Nebula

Ah yes
in the soft town streets
and in the airliner's seats
a lover of unquiet turns on a tape recorder
and a Belgian girl with a Dürer wig
sings like an angel with a childish voice
'Mama can I have that big elephant
over there?'

But of course darling
you can have that big elephant
you can have anything
so long as I am
so long as you are

So long as the lights of town X are there

And while the hostess's public address system
effortlessly crosses the state frontier
the passengers still see the lights of town X
they have not gone out they have not vanished into the irretrievable
the outskirts of town X have passed on the baton
to the outskirts of another town X
the haloes of their lights are gently touching
light holding light
as people hold hands

in this Europe overcrowded with neighbours
like a summer beach
upon this beautiful inhabited Earth

whose nights do not belong to murderers
but to lovers
and dreams

[EO]

Nocturnal Sounds – Interference

They sound briefly and vanish
long before the first guttural shrieks of birds
the nocturnal sounds in the ether under Prague's Gothic vaulting
they vanish and reappear
like inevitable refrains
they're drowned by more aggressive sounds –

some distant signals of Orient Expresses
the squealing brakes of cars
someone's shout
someone's vain calling
for love
or for life

nocturnal clusters and medleys of sounds
a desperate hand vainly
scanning the dial of radio stations
on our continent
on our planet:
Come to me
Put your mouth on my lips

Where are you my near voice
Where are you music of my real heart

[EO]

Goethe in Marienbad

Forests of baptised springs
and heathen grass

Amidst inspiring green
like an opal jewel

like a tortoise-shell cameo
her naked body

Rain and sun   Angels
furiously grind their platinum teeth

Ah yes   Once more
to lose one's soul

One final time
to nibble the marble that is coming alive

The flesh that smoothly flows
like a verse

Go mad   Grow beautiful   Turn young like a phoenix
in that alchemy of a burning crotch

Ah!   Ulrike von Levetzow
is quietly happy

Quietly happily she caresses
the weary white chest of the poet

And the great geologist and great expert on light
already knows – after tomorrow comes the Devil

to claim his due   The final signature:
longing for the sharp points of breasts

shooting up straight towards the lips
like a suicide's pistol

There'll be no need to slash the wrist
with a sharp penknife

The unmetaphorical
gushing of tubercular blood

[EO]

Star Wars

Who are these creatures
creeping through the diamond darkness
as from the fourth dimension of fear

Who are these faces straight from hallucinations
with eyes full of sulphur
and the purple teeth of vampires

Whose are these android tentacles
as hard as flint and as slippery as jelly
these floating membranes and radiation shields

Who are these winged spider-like creatures
weaving an explosive interplanetary web
from the grey hairs of our anxiety

Whence come all these satanic obsessions
of Hieronymus Bosch and Francisco Goya
these midnight companions of Salvador Dalí

Where are they aiming for, these mythical hybrids
with their genius-like crystal brains
and radiation-proof claws

Who are these non-Biblical prophets
looking upon the stinking human mud
with radar and laser eyes

Who are these super-earthly creatures
watchfully throbbing and stirred up
like spreading vortices

Who are these anti-humanoids
in whose dreams thunders like a symphony
an infinite radiational annihilation

Who are they, above our heads
above our roofs above our tree-tops
above our clouds above our mountain peaks

above our Earth the Moon and Mars
and above Venus and above our Sun
above our living galaxy

above our torment and our joy
and above the vulnerability
of chlorophyll and human lungs and hearts

Who are these merciless computers
whose iridium beaks are open wide
whose pores exude nerve-paralysing gas

Who are these skeletal players of bone flutes
those mad bellow-pumpers of nuclear organs
bewitched by the mirror of the Apocalypse

Who are these creatures
creeping through the diamond darkness
as from the fourth dimension of fear

juggling their suicidal smiles
digging their razor fingernails
into our lips and sleeping eye-lids

Who is it up there in the cosmic cold
that pythically grins at us, a monocle
in his glass eye

Who is it rose on the eruption of fossils
from the depths of the Marianas Trench
from the depths of primordial memory in the anti-universe

Who are who are these creatures
creeping through the diamond darkness
as from the fourth dimension of fear

A dead biological branch
an indecipherable diary of a schizophrenic
full of his babblings and of meaningless lines

here under the heaven of gods and astrophysics
where persistently as grass survives
the wish to live to live to love and live

the unalterable
the unconquerable
genetic code of mankind

[EO]

Bower near the Fountain

Here are the nostalgic colours of autumn
or the matutinal hues of spring

Here no wintry death
and no summer with naked burlesque

Here moving silence here contemplation
here departure into sheltered glow

Here only trembling feelings
full of soft flutes – Philemon and Baucis

Only above us
the ride of the Valkyries those goddesses of endless wars

Only above us
Goethe's mists of blood and Mephistopheles

Here in the gentle twilight
we stitch our masks

[EO]

The 1985 Nobel Prize

Icebergs not only cross the Titanic's path
Icebergs float down the lips of the thirsty
Oh Saudi Arabia Australia Africa
to find safe harbours
here on this childishly imperfect planet
where the colossal masses of ice
might anchor and thaw
the water which people are longing to drink
pure
almost unreal

because a suitable iceberg measures 240 metres
but as a rule shows above the surface
by barely one-tenth of its height

Scientists not only receive Nobel Prizes
in the fireworks of flash bulbs
scientists grope laboriously in the elusive droplet of Earth
scientists break their fingernails
on the black crystal of the Universe
Scientists fall through the immeasurable time of the microcosm
        and macrocosm
as through an opalescent starry well
at whose bottom trembles
sunlight, a tear and a stone
come alive in man
for they are the angels on the point of the needle
of knowledge

while we the milling billions
of Whitman's blades of grass
hardly notice the violin in Einstein's hands

Ah yes Klaus von Kitzing
is a young physicist with a boyish grin
a charming wife Renate
and three delightful children
But the discovery of the quantum Hall effect...?

How reassuring and cosy it sounds
that Klaus von Kitzing has shown
that physics is still an experimental science –
even his four-year-old son Thomas
is experimentally wrecking his first alarm-clock
and eight-year-old Christina is trying her luck
in an amusing computer game of space war

Professor Jerome Karle and Herbert Aaron Hauptman
of the Naval Research Laboratory in Washington
were not born near Poznan as Klaus von Kitzing was
at the end of the Second World War
but in the safety of Brooklyn and New York
at the end of the first world war
Ah yes Professor Hauptman creates
unique artistic works from coloured glass
arranged according to mathematical principles of symmetry
and theoretical crystallography

ah yes let's go and see the exhibition with the two professors –
but their direct x-ray analysis
of crystal structures...?
Doesn't it enable us to dissect the guts of molecules
with an accuracy a thousand times greater
than the distance between the atoms?
Really?   Oh yes   Of course
Diffraction   Oh yes I understand   A symbolic summation
Oh yes   Yes of course
with an accuracy a thousand times greater...

Ah geniuses with your violins
how very close to poetry you are
how close to dreams and metaphors
how close to psychotic fog
but how you nevertheless drift away from us
on the foam-tipped waves of the Rhine
beyond the incalculable Lorelei
We only listen
in case a word rings out like a flash
from metals and plastic instruments
into man's sinking heart

But the other laureates too are all smiles –
professors Joseph L. Goldstein and Michael S. Brown
from the University of Texas at Dallas
they believe they can help save the heart
ours and theirs

their magic in the secret world of hypercholesterolemy
is not only hard to pronounce
but again
no more comprehensible to pcople like us
than the writing of an autumn gale

Ah yes they're smiling
remote from us and close to us
thcy're smiling full of shrieking fear
for the heart and the brain the lung and the liver
of this still immature planet

they're smiling
across the invisible sharp edge of horror like the man
who signed his last precise report
without academic titles
in Prague in January:
Jaroslav Seifert

Ah yes let us return to the heart
which today even poets know
by the frightening name of myocardia
because just now two cardiologists
the American professor Bernard Lown
and the Soviet acadcmician Yevgeny Chazov
received the last of the Nobel Prizes
the Peace Prize
on behalf of the International Movement of Doctors
for the Prevention of Nuclear War

Why do 140,000 doctors issue a proclamation?
Because every second a child is dying
who could not be inoculated
Because every minute the world is spending
nearly one and a half million dollars on nuclear weapons
as against three dollars (in words: three dollars) on research
into cardiac arrest

Ah yes the Hiroshima bomb may be called a child's toy
by comparison with a megaton bomb
where will there be a safe Brooklyn
where a cosy spot or children's eyes like marguerites
on a festive table?
What Salvador Dalí will paint
a burning giraffe
a burning swan burning steel burning people
a vitrifying desert and heavenward spurting
stone blocks of ziggurats?

With infinite difficulty is the world learning its lesson
To have enough time
Else mythological gods will be the only survivors
with memories that will terrify them
and which they nevertheless will call up
like a man who looking into a mirror
is desperately choking himself

With infinite pain is the world being born
to wiser hope

[EO]

Berlin – Alexanderplatz

In the colourful autumn afternoon
the Alexanderplatz is in bloom in the eyes of the children
who hang around the fountain without a care in the world

American tank crews with cameras
and British motorised infantrymen in kilts
make in good order for the Hotel Stadt Berlin
to treat themselves to an off-duty drink on the top floor
make sure they buy plush teddy-bears for their girl friends
and through the nearby Checkpoint Charlie
get back to Barracks before retreat is sounded

Tourists from Prague try to make up their minds
in front of the department store
while lovers with bluish-green hair
insatiably greet each other under the clock
just as in the old days

Ah yes, the old days are ever-present
and not only in eternally repeated love –
behind the gleaming slabs of the new buildings
creep shadows of past horrors
the torsos and the ruins into which war had turned
Döblin's old much-loved Alex

Oh what a sooty spring that must have been –
hundreds of thousands digging around in
the smouldering remains of their city

How empty must have been their eyes
Ah yes, those eyes of long ago
The eyes of Carthagenians on the last day of Carthage
The eyes of Babylonians as the armoured chariots
rolled over them

In the Pergamon Museum
the ancient Babylonian kings and gods
have curious ornaments on their hands
perhaps wrist-watches perhaps star compasses

but they're not looking at them
their ancient eyes are fixed on the distance
at the stars or at us
They calculate our time

And in the gallery near by
the colours of the Expressionists explode
The card players in Otto Dix's picture
leer out with their tin jaws and teeth
beckon to us with their tin fingers:
We have come back from the World War
we are the lucky ones we have survived

The marble girl in the garden of the villa
now full of poets will she survive a war?
From the apple tree all covered in golden rennets
sepia-hued leaves drop into the statue's lap
like silent messages
Will any of our messages survive a war?

From the viewing deck of the television tower
from 203 metres up
you observe pedestrians like warrior ants
you observe the cars like remote-controlled
miniature models
you observe the neon lights awakening from their daytime sleep
like glowing eye-shadow or costume jewellery
but you also observe the white wall
which cuts through this divided city
just as those countless other walls and frontiers
cut up our planet
as though someone were dissecting it
on some cosmic operating table

Dusk is falling on the Alexanderplatz
Tomorrow the writers of poetry
will once again discuss the state of the world
between the wilted rhododendrons
and a bed of brilliant asters
again they'll turn their anxious eyes
to the nudity of the marble nymph

Except that statues have no answers
Statues themselves are answer and memento
But do we understand them?
Or are we unaware
that even that strange Berliners' *Tschüss*
was once the French *adieu?*

[EO]

Dying of Franz Kafka at the Kierling Sanatorium

Laughter sun   Silence
Shapely mountain peaks
like a postcard

They've brought him strawberries
refreshing as the lips
of the first love he didn't kiss

And now
he can't swallow
Looks at them   And smiles

that gentle smile from the Book of Esther
He's going home   To Prague
and his marble table

in the snug half-light of the Lesser Town Café
or rather
to the heady hill-slope greenery

of the Nebozízek wine tavern   From the funicular
lovers quicken step
The froth on the beer shines like snow

Above a summer-lit meadow in Brescia
Blériot in his monoplane dips a wing
A Lombardy princess waves a white hand

That was his dying
How good it was here with you
Despite everything   And our thanks

[JM/IM]

Sleep after the Challenger Exploded

Night full of wings
night of the stars' exodus
night of anxiety anxiety

That lily-like longing
and eyes with the promise of dream
then tomorrow...tomorrow

Ah Rainer Maria

Why aren't you sleeping friend when you know
you need more of it
like the flowers

Even the breeze is mute   Then the thunder and the particles
as the planet's heart collapses like a house
Implacable crystals of grief

Go to sleep friend   Try to stave off the noose
of the obsessive film –
that spectral drawn-out burst of the glare

that inferno
above which nothingness
flutters like infinity

Here in Prague full of swans
wild duck gulls and creatures
of forgotten name

I watch the take-off
and
fall

I can't picture horror like Dante
Alighieri
But it's within me

because I knew you
you the vowed
long-reaching human eyes

Where are you bound
in that apocalyptic laughter
of fire

the fourth dimension
where you'll find us
wiser

or
simply
there?

[JM/IM]

Mozart: Requiem

(on the birth of my grandson Christopher)

So you've come to me
through the diamond dust of the universe
little pilgrim
all that unending distance
from the galaxy Makarian 348
through the despairing
estrangement of the stars
but what does it mean
I ask your all-seeing eyes
your scallop-shell soles
what are those 300 million light-years
what are they to us who die
with one hope
that you'll keep returning to us for ever
child

Is there only black light
where you come from?
Only wailing only kisses
between nothingness and nothingness?
Only the unimaginable?

Or joy
like radiation entering
the bone's last molecule?
What's it like where you come from
child?

Ah yes
there are transparent
ice rocks spurting fire
like a flame-thrower
ah yes
our hair to be our hands and eyes to be
keep fearful watch there
from the phosphorescent earth
and instantly wilt

ah yes
child
But what is the truth?

Beyond grief
beyond galactic lament?

Since you've arrived
my pilgrim
in these labyrinths
these lairs and genetic ciphers
where I have to live
like a mouse on the run
where I have to grow
like any other crystal
since you've arrived

answer me

in a word

[JM/IM]

144

Day and Night in Karlovy Vary

I. *The Square*

From the marble Elephant Café
on swift feet
as from a marble crypt
on the graceful legs of the dead
    fleeing faster than light
      from their forgotten rotting bodies
legs like the purple of unease melting
    into a Salvador Dalí painting
      and into the dreams of the sixteen-year-old Jean Arthurs
      the poets of world-weary teenage boys
on the legs of girls now leaving
the marble crypt of the café
so my loves escape headlong
through the paranoid mist of the thermal springs
into a river full of amber fish
and transparent pink and vermilion fish
and return upstream
faster than light like all things
    gone into the past
swift as the irrevocable blood lost in my grief
swift as pain that shoots us
like rabbits like chimeras like vermin
like sixteen-year-old poets

Ah town
inaccessible as a crypt
to sixteen-year-olds
town
mouldering over my memories
like the branch of a fragrant blossoming poisonous tree
holding the remnants of the tiny bones
of a frail corbie
    pecked to death long ago

Ah   town where as in a coma I struggle for breath
    with my memories
like a three-legged wolf

in his bloody tracks
He to breath his last
And I?

2. *Goethe Prospect*

Where is the stone
where is the tree
where is the message
of Thomas Wolfe
where is the cave
in which distant childhood fawns on us
with a kindly eye like an octopus
where is the stone
where is that star
and where are you
lassie not yet run wild
to guide me
step by step
to a happy death

3. *The Park*

That girl hidden in a lair of blossoms
like in the chlorophyll fearful
arbour of a Grimm brothers' dream
ah childhood hidden
behind the snowy filigree of roofs

How silver and green you are
little mermaid in the park
How far it is to Copenhagen
how near to gentle Christian Andersens

How near I still am
to returning to myself

Only that the chimeras in me
bare their teeth with tender malice
only that the wolf in my heart
devoured me long ago

146

4. *Night*

'Only love'
yes child only love
on this dance floor
that shines more bloodily
than the aged vermilion fish in the spa's river
only love –
frenzy of feet
frenzy of small feet of children's feet pitter-patter
yes like make-believe

And as in a fairy-tale
pitter-patter I was suddenly beside you
yet in a moment back again
'I just know you say I love you...'
– how the banalities intertwine
like sepia like fraternising drunkards
while on the parquet
your bare white
child's foot
suddenly glows blood-red

Above the bar the rambler flowers' green tendrils
stifle their quiet laugh
encircling like lovers
the dark green bottles of wine

How far your joy flew away
on foot-soles of swansdown

5. *Dream*

Like a silver-furred animal
with eyes from another galaxy
like a small breathing creature
we meet in a dream –
creature of the galaxies
that escapes before we wake and doesn't reveal
its name
you flee from me

eyelids locked
to the seventh turn of the make-believe key
and never never tell
your real name

ah swan
song of the lakes
tracks in the stone
imprinted as in still live lava

This is your hand on my heart
hand in which the wild blood flows and pulses
and this is my hand on your heart
(in which the wild blood flows and pulses)
one sad hand
on one live heart

ah child
my frail footbridge
to the child in me

6. *Awakening – Visit like from a UFO*

A normal autumn
                    Wind
the man comes and says:
Good afternoon my girl
But how you've grown
soon I'll have to call you Miss
as they say

And opening her big eyes wide
she stares at him
keys in her timid left fist:
Mummy isn't home yet
mister

[JM/IM]

Falling into the Night

Into the black moss
into the tender depths of night

Into the rasping sharpness of reeds
into the edges of night

Into the Grimms' shadowy ferns
into your Midsummer night

On to the razor-edge into the glass into the claws
into the night in me

[JM/IM]

The Amusement Park on a Winter's Night

Night swirling night stirred
by drowning hands
and drowning voices

Darkness like a last scream
Like a racing
black flame

Where are they flying to
these silent pillars of dust
these wailing fragments of forgotten sentences

Where are they coming from
these garlands of desperate leaves
these Chagall lovers and horses

these all-knowing
sellers of burning laughter
and sweaty mother-of-pearl

Night bleeding
night skinned to the bone
Night as in a beast's entrails

Darkness like the rustle
of funereal sand
Darkness as if poisoned in distant childhood

Towards whom are they sprouting
these purple tendrils of arms
those white dossiers like milk-teeth

What are they inflated by
those tough tarpaulins of dreams
like indifferent stones they fall from the stars

and under what heat does the grille melt
in the aviaries of poisoned birds
Who is it threatens from the bottom of bottomless time

Night grinding like a transmission
night panting night trampling
night girded with spiked wings

Darkness like a cathedral
with an organ sonata by Paul Hindemith
Darkness like the sunny eyes of death

[EO]

Childhood as in a Dream

In the soft shade of a larch
Under the floor
of a thundering toboggan

Ah yes in the bullet-proof shade
of a fairy tale book   In the machinery
of mechanical wells and mountains

With flying eyes   In the embrace
of azure waves   On the eternal road
from the Apennines to the Andes

Head in sky-towering heather
amidst flies and crystals
on the palm golden fairies overflowing

The snake-bitten snake prince   Alone
in the rain of meteorites   Alone
in the blood of happenings

[EO]

Heidenröslein

So softly the song woven by
the white spinet

So considerately it caresses it
and leads it under the brocade canopy

to a silken turtle-dove bed
And the song lies down here with Margaretha

removes the wig of its hair
the rosy skin mask of its skin

removes the golden thimble
and with it the childish conjuring magic

The gates of Valhalla are wide open
the gnomes choke with the laughter of triangles

The doctor of all law and philosophy
having grown old in a single night

already weighs a shovel and a spade
already in his mind builds dykes and digs canals

already ploughs all Friesia over
He'll never find her grave

[EO]

Bus Passing a Cemetery

Some ancient Thracians
some Czechs
some Basques
Rhaetians or their dogs

Crowd together
elbow their way forward
beside their graves

They want to be heard:

How are we
we passers-by

How are we really
we the ever thirsty
we the strugglers
how is it with us
who still march on

Better not ask
friends

[JM/IM]

Meteor

A starless night above Prague
The hours between the last song of the drunkards
and the first bark of the high-flats dog
Nineveh

> Dream: an evenly flowing river
> and above it rocks make-believe houses
> Pleasant rolling country
> as in a western

> Ah a river lined with caraway
> a river
> with the exquisite poisonous scent of dill
> on the soles of very old
> and very small children
> Nineveh

A starless night above Prague
The hour of whispering flowers in a room
Hour of stress on the phone
talking to the Samaritans

A starless night above Prague
But in the sky
the glowing sickle of the moon
glowing like live silver
in the sinister flash of a camera

Ah yes under the sky
a fluorescent lamp pallid like Readers of Dostoyevsky
under the sky
a lonely window gleams in the dark
someone's long secret spirit
offering itself with a sudden cry
to anyone

A starless night above Prague
Night vibrating with electric sounds
Puffing of distant trains

wail of the last taxi
Rustle and clatter   Humming of the blood and wheels
wearing themselves out on the roadway

A starless night above Prague
and at this moment
this moment seemingly void
like the stillness of age-old menhirs
a meteor approaches
perhaps a mythical longed-for envoy
maybe only a particle
from a cosmic storm
a cooling fragment struck
from the hydraulic anvil of the gods

A starless night above Prague
The meteor flies on
on impact it will die
become a burnt-out porous stone

but it flies on
bright as the moon's glowing sickle
like the ruby lights on the roofs of high-rise blocks
that flash a possible message
and astonish night passengers
eyeing the flickering lights of a passing plane
which they take for galactic probes
or telecommunication satellites
somewhere in the dark and icy spaces

A starless night above Prague
but the one and only morning star then springs out
like a silver shot
like the needle point beckoning junkies
for a final heavenly trip

The only star
far from the sickle moon
in the grey-blue sky
which is suddenly split by a jagged line
of poisonous pink waste from the plane
like a crude surgical section

An almost starless night above Prague
The aniline pink loop
slowly dissolves
in the decadent sky
matted like a lamb's fleece tinted hip-rose
like the hint of a *vin rosé* coloured noose
around the sickle moon
curved softly white
like a child's footsole

Noose unfinished
Challenge
Nineveh

Night above Prague
The meteor falls
Headstrong as in love
Headlong like
to a futile death

[JM/IM]

OTHER CZECH POETS FROM BLOODAXE

MIROSLAV HOLUB: *Poems Before & After: Collected English Translations*
Translated by Ian & Jarmila Milner, Ewald Osers and George Theiner
Holub's most important book: his early work from his Penguin *Sel-ected Poems* and Bloodaxe's *The Fly* with the later poetry of his other Bloodaxe selection, *On the Contrary*. 'A laying bare of things, not so much the skull beneath the skin, more the brain beneath the skull; the shape of relationships, politics, history; the rhythms of affection and disaffection; the ebb and flow of faith, hope, violence, art' – SEAMUS HEANEY.

MIROSLAV HOLUB: *The Jingle Bell Principle*
Translated by James Naughton
Miroslav Holub has been called 'one of the half-dozen most imp-ortant poets writing anywhere' (TED HUGHES). In the scientific community his renown rests on such works as *Immunology of Nude Mice*. In Czechoslovakia he also writes a highly popular magazine column. When Holub was a "non-person", these "column articles" weren't published under his own name, but everyone knew who'd written them because the style was immediately recognisable as his: a cross between Flann O'Brien and Jonathan Swift, with a dash of *Tristram Shandy*...the Beachcomber of Wenceslas Square.

SYLVA FISCHEROVÁ: *The Tremor of Racehorses: Selected Poems*
Translated by Jarmila & Ian Milner
'She does not play at being a woman poet, she is one, and her poems reflect the atmosphere and conditions of her homeland' – MIROSLAV HOLUB. 'An underlying satirical vision of considerable edge' – JOHN LUCAS, *New Statesman*

THE NEW CZECH POETRY, *translated by Ewald Osers*
Jaroslav Čejka, Michael Černík and Karel Sýs: three leading Czech poets from the generation after Holub.

VLADIMIR JANOVIC: *The House of the Tragic Poet*
Translated by Ewald Osers
The last days of Pompeii are recreated in this gripping epic by a leading Czech poet.

For a complete catalogue of Bloodaxe titles, please write to:
Bloodaxe Books Ltd, P.O. Box 1SN, Newcastle upon Tyne NE99 1SN.

AUTHORS PUBLISHED BY
BLOODAXE BOOKS

FLEUR ADCOCK
GÖSTA ÅGREN
ANNA AKHMATOVA
GILLIAN ALLNUTT
SIMON ARMITAGE
NEIL ASTLEY
ATTILA the STOCKBROKER
ANNEMARIE AUSTIN
SHIRLEY BAKER
MARTIN BELL
CONNIE BENSLEY
STEPHEN BERG
ATTILIO BERTOLUCCI
YVES BONNEFOY
KARIN BOYE
KAMAU BRATHWAITE
BASIL BUNTING
CIARAN CARSON
JOHN CASSIDY
AIMÉ CÉSAIRE
SID CHAPLIN
RENÉ CHAR
GEORGE CHARLTON
EILÉAN NÍ CHUILLEANÁIN
KILLARNEY CLARY
BRENDAN CLEARY
JACK CLEMO
HARRY CLIFTON
JACK COMMON
STEWART CONN
NOEL CONNOR
DAVID CONSTANTINE
CHARLOTTE CORY
JENI COUZYN
HART CRANE
ADAM CZERNIAWSKI
FRED D'AGUIAR
PETER DIDSBURY
STEPHEN DOBYNS
MAURA DOOLEY
KATIE DONOVAN
JOHN DREW
IAN DUHIG
HELEN DUNMORE
STEPHEN DUNSTAN
JACQUES DUPIN
G.F. DUTTON
LAURIS EDMOND
ALISTAIR ELLIOT
STEVE ELLIS
ODYSSEUS ELYTIS
EURIPIDES
DAVID FERRY
EVA FIGES
SYLVA FISCHEROVÁ
TONY FLYNN

VICTORIA FORDE
TUA FORSSTRÖM
JIMMY FORSYTH
LINDA FRANCE
ELIZABETH GARRETT
ARTHUR GIBSON
PAMELA GILLILAN
ANDREW GREIG
CHRIS GREENHALGH
JOHN GREENING
PHILIP GROSS
JOSEF HANZLÍK
TONY HARRISON
GEOFF HATTERSLEY
ANNE HÉBERT
W.N. HERBERT
HAROLD HESLOP
DOROTHY HEWETT
SELIMA HILL
FRIEDRICH HÖLDERLIN
MIROSLAV HOLUB
FRANCES HOROVITZ
DOUGLAS HOUSTON
JOHN HUGHES
PAUL HYLAND
STEPHEN KNIGHT
PHILIPPE JACCOTTET
KATHLEEN JAMIE
VLADIMÍR JANOVIC
B.S. JOHNSON
LINTON KWESI JOHNSON
JOOLZ
JENNY JOSEPH
SYLVIA KANTARIS
JACKIE KAY
BRENDAN KENNELLY
SIRKKA-LIISA KONTTINEN
JEAN HANFF KORELITZ
DENISE LEVERTOV
HERBERT LOMAS
MARION LOMAX
EDNA LONGLEY
FEDERICO GARCÍA LORCA
GEORGE MacBETH
PETER McDONALD
DAVID McDUFF
MEDBH McGUCKIAN
MAIRI MacINNES
CHRISTINE McNEILL
OSIP MANDELSTAM
GERALD MANGAN
E.A. MARKHAM
WILLIAM MARTIN
GLYN MAXWELL
HENRI MICHAUX
ADRIAN MITCHELL

JOHN MONTAGUE
EUGENIO MONTALE
DAVID MORLEY
RICHARD MURPHY
HENRY NORMAL
SEAN O'BRIEN
JULIE O'CALLAGHAN
JOHN OLDHAM
OTTÓ ORBÁN
MICHEAL O'SIADHAIL
RUTH PADEL
TOM PAULIN
GYÖRGY PETRI
TOM PICKARD
JILL PIRRIE
SIMON RAE
DEBORAH RANDALL
IRINA RATUSHINSKAYA
MARIA RAZUMOVSKY
PETER REDGROVE
ANNE ROUSE
CAROL RUMENS
LAWRENCE SAIL
EVA SALZMAN
PETER SANSOM
SAPPHO
DAVID SCOTT
JO SHAPCOTT
SIR ROY SHAW
ELENA SHVARTS
MATT SIMPSON
LEMN SISSAY
DAVE SMITH
KEN SMITH
SEAN MAYNE SMITH
STEPHEN SMITH
EDITH SÖDERGRAN
PIOTR SOMMER
MARIN SORESCU
LEOPOLD STAFF
PAULINE STAINER
EIRA STENBERG
MARTIN STOKES
RABINDRANATH TAGORE
JEAN TARDIEU
D.M. THOMAS
R.S. THOMAS
TOMAS TRANSTRÖMER
MARINA TSVETAYEVA
MIRJAM TUOMINEN
FRED VOSS
NIGEL WELLS
C.K. WILLIAMS
JOHN HARTLEY WILLIAMS
JAMES WRIGHT
BENJAMIN ZEPHANIAH

For a complete catalogue of books published by Bloodaxe, pleaee write to:
Bloodaxe Books Ltd, P.O. Box 1SN, Newcastle upon Tyne NE99 1SN.